Little Kitchen of Horrors

HiDEOUSLY DELICIOUS RECIPES THAT DISGUST AND DELIGHT

Ali Vega

Lerner Publications ◆ Minneapolis

CONTENTS

GROSSIFY YOUR FOOD

Nasty Names

Making food look disgusting is an important part of any revolting recipe. But a good gross-out name can also change an everyday edible into something truly nasty. An egg turns into a slimy eyeball, ketchup becomes blood, and hot dogs start looking a lot like severed fingers. A terrible name can turn any recipe into something gag-worthy.

As you cook, look at the ingredients in each recipe. Do any of them inspire you to create new nasty names? Be sure to announce the title of each disgusting dish you serve. Your guests' looks of horror are half the fun!

Sickening Setups

A stomach-churning appearance and nauseating name are not all that will make your party foods as horrifying as they can be. Presentation is also important. Fun props can make your food seem extra revolting. Create swarms of fake insects crawling across the table. Maybe you'd like to serve your food with toilet-paper napkins. And there's nothing like clean bandages dipped in cherry juice to make a table look especially creepy. Make sure to sanitize props before using them. And remove the props from the food before serving your guests. Keep things fun and delicious without putting your diners in danger.

Before You GeT STaRTeD

Cook Safely! Creating revolting recipes means using different kitchen tools and appliances. These items can be very hot or sharp. Make sure to get an adult's help whenever making a recipe that requires use of an oven, stove, or knife.

Be a Smart Chef! Cooking horrifying foods can be messy. Ask an adult for permission before starting a new cooking project. Then make sure you have a clean workspace. Wash your hands often while cooking. If you have long hair, be sure to tie it back. Make sure your guests don't have any food allergies before cooking. Adjust the recipes if you need to. Make sure your petrifying party foods are safe to eat!

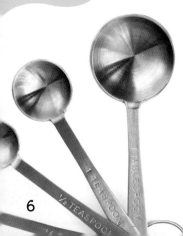

Tools You'll Need

Cooking can involve special tools and appliances. You will need the following items for these disgusting recipes:

- food processor or blender
- freezer
- microwave
- mixer or hand mixer
- oven
- refrigerator
- slow cooker
- stove or hot plate

METRIC CONVERSION CHART

Use this handy chart to convert recipes to the metric system. If you can't find the conversion you need, ask an adult to help you find an online calculator!

STANDARD	METRIC
¼ teaspoon	1.2 milliliters
½ teaspoon	2.5 ml
¾ teaspoon	3.7 ml
1 teaspoon	5 ml
2 teaspoons	10 ml
1 tablespoon	15 ml
¼ cup	59 ml
⅓ cup	79 ml
½ cup	118 ml
⅔ cup	158 ml
¾ cup	177 ml
1 cup	237 ml

150 degrees Fahrenheit	66 degrees Celsius
300°F	149°C
350°F	177°C
400°F	204°C

1 ounce	28 grams
1 fluid ounce	30 milliliters
1 inch	2.5 centimeters
1 pound	0.5 kilograms

REPULSIVE BREAKFASTS

Do you dream of starting your day with an oozing bowl of brains for breakfast? Have you ever wished for a serving of slimy eyeballs alongside your cereal and toast? These revolting breakfast recipes may seem super gross. But don't be afraid to try them all.

The key to these breakfast dishes is that they are actually delicious. Your friends and family will love gulping down scrumptious chunky snot smoothies, mouthwatering blood-and-guts pastries, and many more tasty, horrifying breakfasts!

SNOT SMOOTHIE

Whip up a quick and healthful mucus shake for breakfast. Those extra-thick globs of nose juice wash right down!

Ingredients

2 ripe bananas
½ cup milk
½ cup vanilla yogurt
1 cup cut-up or canned fruit, such as peaches, pears, or melons
½ cup sunflower or pumpkin seeds
1 handful spinach leaves
½ avocado
½ cup ice cubes

Tools

• knife
• cutting board
• blender
• measuring cups

Serves: 1–2
Preparation Time: 30 minutes

1. Peel and cut up the bananas, and put them in the blender.

2. Add the milk and yogurt to the blender.

3. Add the fruit, seeds, spinach, and avocado to the blender.

4. With an adult's help, turn on the blender and pulse 7 to 10 times, or until the ingredients are blended.

5. Add the ice cubes, and pulse some more. Stop when the mixture is smooth and creamy. No tissues needed for this delicious drink.

TIP

No dairy, no problem! Substitute almond milk, rice milk, or soy milk for dairy milk.

11

BOWL OF BRAINS

Become extra smart by eating brains for breakfast. Don't worry about lumps in this nutritious dish.

Ingredients

¼ cup milk, plus a few extra splashes for serving
2 cups rolled oats
1 15-ounce can pumpkin puree
1 teaspoon vanilla extract
2 teaspoons pumpkin pie spice
2 tablespoons maple syrup, plus more for serving
¼ teaspoon salt
1 apple
¼ cup almonds
½ cup raspberry jam

Tools

- saucepan
- measuring cups
- measuring spoons
- mixing spoon
- peeler
- knife
- cutting board
- serving bowls
- small bowl

Serves: 4
Preparation Time: 10–30 minutes

1. In a saucepan over high heat, bring 3¾ cups water to a boil with an adult's help. Add ¼ cup milk and the oats. Then reduce the temperature to medium. Cook for 1 to 2 minutes.

2. Add the pumpkin puree, vanilla extract, pumpkin pie spice, 2 tablespoons maple syrup, and salt to the saucepan. Stir together.

2

3. Peel and chop the apple. Add it to the saucepan and stir. Cook for 3 to 10 minutes, or until the oats are cooked. Remove the saucepan from the heat.

4. Chop the almonds into small pieces.

3

5. Scoop the oatmeal into bowls, and garnish each one with nuts, a splash of milk, and a bit of maple syrup.

6. Put the raspberry jam in a small bowl. Add 1 or 2 tablespoons of water, and stir until runny. Drizzle the jam over the brains for a bloody garnish. Then watch your guests grimace as they dig into these appetizing brains.

5

TIP

Make your own pumpkin pie spice. Just mix together 2 teaspoons ground cinnamon and ¼ teaspoon each of ground ginger, nutmeg, allspice, and ground cloves.

BLOODY EYEBALL EGGS

These slimy fried eyes will stare back at hungry diners!

Ingredients

2 sausage links
1 tablespoon butter
4 eggs
¼ cup ketchup

Tools

- measuring cups
- frying pan
- spatula
- knife
- cutting board
- serving plates
- table knife

Serves: 2–4
Preparation Time: 30 minutes

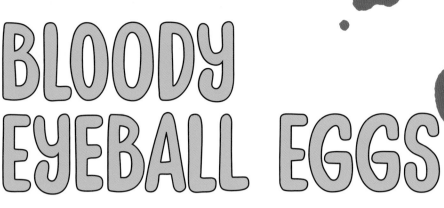

1. Put ¼ cup water and the sausages in the frying pan. With an adult's help, cook the sausages for 6 to 8 minutes over medium-high heat. Turn the sausages, and cook for 6 to 8 more minutes or until done. Remove the sausages, and let them cool.

2. Cut the tips off each sausage. Each tip should be about ¼ inch long.

3. Place the butter in the frying pan, and melt it over medium heat. Then crack an egg and drop it near the edge of the pan. Repeat with another egg.

4. Cook both eggs for 5 minutes, or until the whites are cooked through and the yolks are soft.

5. Remove each egg with a spatula and put it on a plate. Repeat steps 3 through 5 until the other eggs are cooked.

6. Use a table knife to decorate your eyeballs with ketchup veins. Then place a sausage tip in the middle of each egg for the pupil. Cut up the rest of the sausages to serve on the side. Your guests will gobble up these bloody eyeballs!

TIP

For a vegetarian breakfast, use two black olives for pupils instead of the sausage tips.

GREEN ZOMBIE FLESH AND OOZE

French toast becomes flaky zombie skin in this deadly dish! Don't forget the creamy zombie pus for dipping.

Ingredients

Ooze
3 ripe bananas
1 tablespoon maple syrup
1 teaspoon vanilla extract
1 teaspoon cinnamon
2 handfuls fresh baby spinach leaves
1½ cups milk
4 large slices of bread
2 tablespoons butter

Tools

• measuring spoons
• measuring cups
• blender
• large bowl
• frying pan
• spatula

Serves: 4
Preparation Time: 30–45 minutes

1. Peel the bananas. With an adult's help, blend the bananas, maple syrup, vanilla, cinnamon, spinach, and milk in the blender until mixed. This is your ooze. Measure out ¾ cup of the ooze, and put it in the refrigerator. Pour the rest into a large bowl.

1

2. Soak each piece of bread in the bowl of ooze.

3. Melt the butter in the frying pan over medium heat.

4. Add the ooze-soaked slices of bread to the frying pan. Then cook for 3 to 4 minutes. Using a spatula, turn each slice over, and cook another 2 to 3 minutes. Add a spoonful of ooze to each, and cook for 1 to 2 more minutes.

2

5. Serve each scabby slice of fleshy toast with a heaping side of zombie ooze!

4

CRUSHED BONES

Bloody jam makes these broken bones an extra-sweet breakfast treat!

Ingredients

1 8-count package refrigerated
   cinnamon rolls
½ cup raspberry or
   strawberry jam

Tools

- knife
- cutting board
- baking sheet
- parchment paper
- oven mitts
- measuring cup
- measuring spoons
- serving plate

Serves: 4–6
Preparation Time: 30 minutes

1. Preheat the oven according to the cinnamon roll package. Separate the rolls into sections and unroll them. Cut each section in half.

1

2. Cover a baking sheet with parchment paper. Sculpt each roll section to look like a bone. Place the bones on the baking sheet.

3. Bake the bones for 10 to 12 minutes, or according to the package instructions. With an adult's help, take the baking sheet out of the oven, and let the bones cool.

2

4. Now break the bones. Split them into pieces of various sizes, and add 1 teaspoon of jam to each jagged bone end.

5. Bake the bones another 2 to 3 minutes.

6. Remove the baking sheet from the oven, and put the bones on a serving plate. Drench them in drippy jam blood. Then let diners dig through the wreckage to choose their bones!

4

TIP

To make your bones extra realistic, ask an adult to help you look up bone images online. Shape your bones to look like the ones in the images.

SPIDER EGGS

The spooky spiderwebs in these savory hard-boiled eggs make for a creepy-crawly treat!

Ingredients

1 dozen eggs
1 teaspoon salt
¼ onion
2 teabags black tea
4 tablespoons soy sauce
1 2-inch piece peeled, fresh ginger

Tools

- large stockpot
- measuring spoons
- slotted spoon
- large bowl
- knife
- cutting board

Serves: 3–4
Preparation Time: 2½–3 hours

1. Place the eggs in the stockpot, and cover with cold water. Add the salt. With an adult's help, bring the water to a boil over high heat. Turn the temperature down to medium-low, and simmer for 15 minutes.

1

2. Carefully remove the pot from the heat. Using a slotted spoon, move the eggs to a large bowl, and fill with cool water. Let the eggs cool for 15 to 30 minutes. Ask an adult to help you drain the stockpot.

3. Gently crack each cooled egg on a countertop or table. Crack in several places on each egg. But don't remove the shells from the eggs.

3

4. Put the eggs back in the stockpot and cover them with water again. Chop the onion into small pieces. Add the teabags, soy sauce, ginger, and onion to the stockpot. Bring to a boil over high heat. Turn the temperature down to medium-low, and let the eggs simmer for 1 hour.

5. Carefully remove the pot from the heat and let the eggs cool in the liquid. Peel each egg when cool. Now startle squeamish diners with these web-covered eggs!

4

CLOGGED-DRAIN HAIR CLUMP CEREAL

These cereal stacks look just like matted clumps of hair you might fish out of a clogged drain!

Ingredients

2 tablespoons butter
3 tablespoons honey
1 cup chocolate chips
1 teaspoon vanilla extract
¼ teaspoon salt
3 large shredded wheat bundles
milk, for serving

Tools

- medium saucepan
- measuring spoons
- measuring cups
- mixing spoon
- baking sheet
- waxed paper
- serving bowl

Serves: 4–6
Preparation Time: 1 hour
(15–30 minutes active)

1

1 Melt the butter in a saucepan over medium heat. Add the honey, chocolate chips, vanilla, and salt. Stir until the chocolate is melted and the ingredients are combined and smooth. Remove the pan from heat.

2 Loosen and break up the wheat bundles with clean hands. Then place the bundles in the saucepan with the chocolate mixture. Gently stir until all the shredded wheat is coated with chocolate.

2

3 Line a baking sheet with waxed paper.

4 Scoop similar-sized clumps of the chocolate-coated wheat onto the waxed paper. Let them cool in the refrigerator for 30 to 45 minutes.

5 Your clumps are ready to serve! A swig of milk helps hungry diners wash these hairy tangles down their drains!

4

BLOOD AND GUTS

A terrifying treat for gore-loving guests.

Ingredients

Filling
¾ cup brown sugar
½ cup granulated sugar
1 tablespoon cinnamon
1 tablespoon vanilla extract
½ teaspoon salt
2 tablespoons butter

Dough
2½ cups all-purpose flour, plus
    more for rolling out dough
⅓ cup granulated sugar
1½ teaspoons baking powder
½ teaspoon baking soda
½ teaspoon salt
1 cup buttermilk
4 tablespoons butter, melted
cooking spray

Frosting
4 ounces cream cheese, softened
1 cup powdered sugar
4 tablespoons buttermilk

Sauce
⅔ cup raspberry jam
¼ cup light corn syrup
½ teaspoon liquid red food coloring

Tools

• measuring cups
• measuring spoons
• mixing bowls of various sizes
• mixing spoons
• whisk
• rolling pin
• knife
• cutting board
• 9 x 13-inch baking dish
• oven mitts
• fork
• table knife

Serves: 4–6
Preparation Time: 30–45 minutes

1. Preheat the oven to 425°F. Mix the filling ingredients together in a medium bowl, and set it aside.

1

2. Next, make the dough. In a large bowl, stir together the flour, granulated sugar, baking powder, baking soda, and salt. In a small bowl, whisk the buttermilk and melted butter together. Mix gently with the dry ingredients. Stop as soon as the ingredients are combined. Knead the dough for 1 or 2 minutes. Then divide it into two equal chunks.

3. Sprinkle flour over a clean work surface. Then roll one chunk of dough into a rectangle. It should be a little bigger than a piece of notebook paper. Spread one-half of the filling evenly across dough, leaving space around the edges. Then roll the dough up and pinch the ends. Repeat with the other chunk of dough and the rest of the filling.

3

4. Coat the baking dish with cooking spray. Cut the dough into pieces of many different sizes. These will be your cinnamon rolls. Place the pieces in the baking dish. Scoop 2 tablespoons of jam on top. With an adult's help, bake for 15 to 18 minutes, and remove from oven.

5. Now make the frosting. Put the cream cheese and powdered sugar in a bowl. Blend them with a fork. Add the buttermilk, 1 tablespoon at a time. Spread the frosting on top of the baked rolls.

4

6. Finally, make the sauce. In a small bowl, stir together the rest of the jam, corn syrup, and food coloring. Drizzle the sauce over the warm rolls. These monster guts may look horrifying, but they will taste delicious!

SPOOKY SKULL EGGS

A grinning skeleton egg with a yummy yolk filling makes a tasty treat for breakfast, brunch, or anytime!

Ingredients

1 dozen eggs
1¼ teaspoon salt
½ cup mayonnaise
1 tablespoon mustard
¼ teaspoon pepper
2 teaspoons Worcestershire sauce
1 dash hot sauce
paprika
ketchup, for serving

Tools

- large stockpot
- measuring spoons
- slotted spoon
- mixing bowls, various sizes
- knife
- cutting board
- spoon
- fork
- measuring cups
- drinking straws
- coffee stir straws

Serves: 4–5
Preparation Time: 1 hour

1. Place the eggs in the stockpot and cover with cold water. Add 1 teaspoon salt. With an adult's help, bring to a boil over high heat. Turn the temperature down to medium-low, and simmer for 15 minutes.

2. Carefully remove the pot from heat. Using a slotted spoon, move the eggs to a large bowl, and fill it with cool water. Let the eggs cool for 15 to 30 minutes.

3

3. Crack the eggs and carefully peel them.

4. With an adult's help, slice each egg in half lengthwise, and remove the yolks with a spoon. Put the yolks in a bowl.

5. Mash the yolks together using the back of a fork. Mix in the mayonnaise, mustard, ¼ teaspoon salt, pepper, Worcestershire sauce, and hot sauce. This makes a filling.

4

Skull Eggs continued next page

5

Have an adult help you look up
pictures of skulls online to make
sure yours look realistic.

28

Skull Eggs, continued

6 Scoop 1 tablespoon of filling into each egg white. Sprinkle each egg with paprika. Pair up each egg half with another egg half, so the two halves stick together. The filling should seal them. These are your skulls.

6

7 Using a drinking straw, poke two holes in each egg for eyes.

8 Using the same straw, carefully poke a hole for the nose.

9 Poke small holes using the coffee stir straw to make rows of teeth in each skull.

10 Arrange the skulls on a plate. Drizzle ketchup over them for some extra flare, and dish up your grinning skulls at your next brunch.

7

9

LOATHSOME LUNCHES

You're home on a Saturday and hungry for lunch. You peer into the refrigerator. Eyeballs bobbing in bloody soup stare back at you. A pungent pile of dog doo sits on the second shelf. And look, there are leftovers! Worms writhe under hamburger-bun hats. These lunches might seem fit for a monster. But they are edible and even enjoyable.

These disgusting yet delicious lunch foods are tons of fun to make and serve. So set the table and steel your stomach. It's time for the most sickening, vile lunches you'll ever love to eat!

WRITHING WORM SANDWICHES

Sliced worms topped with bloody barbecue sauce make a squirming sandwich.

Ingredients

6 hot dogs
2 tablespoons cooking oil
½ cup barbecue sauce
6 hamburger buns

Serves: 4–6
**Preparation Time:
10–15 minutes**

Tools

- knife
- cutting board
- measuring spoons
- frying pan
- tongs
- mixing bowl
- measuring cups
- mixing spoon
- oven mitts

1. Preheat the oven to 350°F. Cut each hot dog into five or six wormlike strips.

1

2. With an adult's help, heat the oil in a frying pan over medium heat. Add the strips, and let them sizzle for 2 to 3 minutes.

3. Using tongs, carefully turn each strip over. Then cook them for another 2 minutes. Repeat until the strips begin to crisp and curl. Take the hot dogs out of the frying pan and place in a bowl.

3

4. Cover the hot dogs with the barbecue sauce and stir.

5. Carefully place the buns face down directly on the oven rack. Toast for 3 minutes at 350°F. Have an adult help you remove the buns from the oven.

6. Sandwich several hot dog strips between a top and bottom bun. Repeat to make the remaining sandwiches. Watch squeamish guests squirm as they chomp on their wriggling worms!

4

BLOOD-SOAKED EYEBALL SOUP

Creepy cheese eyeballs peer at diners from a bloody bath of tomato soup.

Ingredients

1 sweet onion
5 tablespoons olive oil
2 minced garlic cloves
2½ tablespoons flour
2 teaspoons dried basil
4 cups vegetable broth
2 28-ounce cans crushed tomatoes
1 tablespoon sugar
½ teaspoon salt
½ teaspoon ground pepper
canned whole black olives
cherry-sized fresh mozzarella balls
pimientos

Tools

- knife
- cutting board
- measuring spoons
- large stockpot with lid
- mixing spoon
- measuring cups
- ladle
- serving bowls

Serves: 4–6
Preparation Time: 1 hour

3

1. With an adult's help, carefully chop the onion into small pieces. Heat the oil in a stockpot over medium heat. Add the chopped onion, and cook for 5 to 7 minutes.

2. Add the garlic to the stockpot, and cook for 3 more minutes, stirring constantly. Add the flour, and stir until it is blended and not lumpy. Stir in the basil, and cook for 2 more minutes.

3. Add the vegetable broth, crushed tomatoes, sugar, salt, and pepper to the stockpot. Stir the mixture until it simmers. Turn the temperature to low, cover the pot, and cook for another 30 minutes.

4. Cut each olive in half. Then use a knife to carefully scoop a small hole out of each mozzarella ball. Place an olive half into the hole to make a pupil. Then add a pimiento to the center of each olive for an iris. The mozzarella balls should look like eyeballs!

5. Ladle the soup into bowls, and add two or three eyeballs to each bowl. Watch your guests enjoy a bloody bowl of warmth and comfort.

4

TIP

For a meatier flavor, try chicken broth instead of the vegetable broth.

TOMBSTONE SANDWICHES

Dig up delicious grilled gravestones with these classic sandwiches!

Ingredients

1 medium bunch kale, washed
1 tablespoon olive oil
¼ teaspoon salt
4 tablespoons butter
8 slices sourdough bread
¼ cup plus 4 teaspoons mustard
4 slices Muenster cheese
8 slices cheddar cheese
8 slices ham

Tools

- knife
- cutting board
- large mixing bowl
- measuring spoons
- baking sheet
- oven mitts
- table knife
- frying pan with lid
- spatula
- small zipper-close plastic bag
- scissors
- serving plate

Serves: 4
Preparation Time: 30–45 minutes

1. Preheat the oven to 350°F. Cut off the kale leaves, and discard the stems. Tear the leaves into 2- to 3-inch pieces. Place the leaves in a bowl, and add the oil. Mix the kale and oil with clean hands until the leaves are completely coated. Then arrange the leaves in a single layer on a baking sheet. Sprinkle with salt. Bake the kale for 8 to 11 minutes, or until crispy.

1

2. Butter one side of each slice of bread. This will be the outer side. Then spread 1 teaspoon of mustard on the other side of each bread slice. Now, layer one slice of bread with one slice of Muenster, two cheddar cheese slices, and two slices of ham. Top with another slice of bread. Repeat until you have used all eight bread slices.

2

3. With an adult's help, heat the frying pan over medium heat. Then place one or two sandwiches in the pan. Place a lid on the pan, and cook for 3 to 4 minutes. Remove the lid, and carefully flip each sandwich. Replace the lid, and cook another 3 to 4 minutes, or until the cheese is melted and the bread is toasted. Repeat until all sandwiches are cooked.

4. Allow the sandwiches cool until they are safe to touch, and put them on a cutting board. Use a table knife to trim each sandwich into a tombstone shape.

3

5. Put the remaining mustard in a plastic bag. Squeeze the mustard down toward a bottom corner. Then trim off the tip of that corner. Squeeze the bag so the mustard comes out as piping. Use the piping to decorate your tombstones.

6. Arrange the crispy kale on the serving plate to look like grass. Then set up the sandwiches on the kale grass. Guests can dig into these gravestones at their own risk!

SUPERSLIMY BAT WINGS

Bite into slime-soaked wings that look like they were just ripped off of bats.

Ingredients

Marinade

4 tablespoons canned black beans
4 cloves minced garlic
4 tablespoons soy sauce
⅔ cup ketchup
4 tablespoons honey
2 tablespoons brown sugar
¼ cup orange juice
½ teaspoon Chinese five-spice
    powder
2 tablespoons sesame oil
blue and green food coloring
4 pounds chicken wings

Tools

- measuring spoons
- fork
- mixing bowls, various sizes
- mixing spoon
- measuring cups
- colander
- large zipper-close plastic bags
- aluminum foil
- 2 baking sheets
- oven mitts
- serving spoon

Serves: 4–6
Preparation Time: 4–5 hours
(30 minutes active)

1. First make the marinade. Mash black beans with a fork in a large mixing bowl. Then stir in the garlic. Add remaining marinade ingredients to the black bean mixture, and stir to combine.

2. Add a few drops of each food coloring to the mixture, and stir until it looks greenish-black in color. Scoop out ½ cup of marinade into a small bowl, and set aside in the refrigerator.

1

3. Rinse chicken wings with water using a colander. Place the wings and marinade in a large plastic bag. Divide the wings and marinade into multiple bags if needed. Seal each bag, and make sure the top is closed tightly before shaking it to coat the wings in the marinade.

4. Place the bag in the refrigerator, and let it sit for 3 or more hours.

3

5. Preheat the oven to 325°F. Put a sheet of aluminum foil on each baking sheet. Arrange the wings on the foil.

6. Bake the wings for 45 minutes to 1 hour. Then serve to your guests with a spoonful of extra marinade for each wing. These beastly bat wings will be so tasty, they will fly off the plates!

5

TIP

Chinese five-spice powder is a blend of cinnamon, cloves, fennel, star anise, and peppercorns. It can be purchased at most grocery stores.

MAGGOT AND BUG SALAD

This creepy-crawly salad will have diners itching to take their first bites.

Ingredients

½ red onion
1 16-ounce can white beans
1 6.5-ounce can marinated
    artichoke hearts

Dressing

1 clove minced garlic
2 tablespoons olive oil
1 tablespoon lemon juice
½ teaspoon dried oregano
½ teaspoon lemon pepper
¼ teaspoon salt
1½ cups uncooked orzo pasta
1 cup crumbled feta cheese
15–20 cherry tomatoes
1 16-ounce can whole black olives

Tools

- knife
- cutting board
- large serving bowl
- measuring spoons
- mixing spoon
- large stockpot
- measuring cups
- colander

Serves: 4
Preparation Time: 1 hour, 30 minutes

1. Carefully chop the onion into ½-inch pieces. Combine the onion, beans, artichoke hearts and their juices, and dressing ingredients into a large bowl. Stir together, and refrigerate for 1 hour.

2. Fill a stockpot with water, and bring to a boil over high heat with an adult's help. Add the orzo pasta and cook for 8 to 10 minutes. Carefully drain the pasta using a colander. Set it aside to cool.

1

3. Add the cooled pasta to the bean mixture, and stir to combine. Stir in the feta cheese.

4. Cut the cherry tomatoes in half the long way. Then cut each half down the middle one more time, stopping just before you reach the top. The tomato should look like a bug's wings!

5. Cut each olive in half the long way. Then cut it in half the long way again. The olives should look like small beetles.

6. Arrange the tomato and olive bugs so they look like they are crawling out of the salad. Then serve this squirming salad to your bug-eyed guests!

3

4

MONSTER-SNOT RAMEN

Slurp up the finger boogers in this slimy ramen!

Ingredients

4 ounces white mushrooms

1 tablespoon sesame oil

4 cloves minced garlic

1 tablespoon freshly grated ginger

4 cups chicken broth

¼ cup soy sauce

3 3-ounce packages dried
ramen noodles (don't use the
seasoning packet)

1 grated carrot

3 cups fresh spinach

8–10 mini hot dogs

½ cup shredded white cheese

2 teaspoons chopped green onions

Tools

- knife
- cutting board
- large stockpot
- grater
- measuring spoons
- mixing spoon
- measuring cups
- medium saucepan
- colander
- ladle
- serving bowls
- fork

Serves: 4
Preparation Time: 20–30 minutes

1. Carefully chop the mushrooms into quarters. With an adult's help, heat the oil in a stockpot over medium heat. Add the garlic and ginger, and cook for 1 to 3 minutes, stirring constantly. Stir in the chicken broth, mushrooms, soy sauce, and 3 cups of water. Bring the mixture to a boil over high heat, and then reduce the temperature to medium-low.

2. Let the mixture simmer for 10 minutes. Add in the ramen noodles and cook for 2 to 3 minutes.

3. Add the carrot and spinach. Cook for 2 more minutes and remove from heat.

4. Fill a saucepan with water, and bring it to a boil over high heat with an adult's help. Meanwhile, shape the hot dog fingers. Use a knife to carefully carve a fingernail into the end of each hot dog. Then make three or four slits halfway down each hot dog to look like knuckles. Boil the hot dogs in the saucepan for 3 to 4 minutes. Remove from heat. Then drain using a colander.

5. Ladle the ramen soup into individual serving bowls. Add a bit of cheese to each bowl. As the cheese melts, swirl it around with a fork to make it look like runny snot.

6. Add two or three hot dogs to each bowl and garnish with the green onions. Then watch your guests relish this revolting ramen.

TIP

If you don't have dried ramen noodles, try using 1 pound of spaghetti noodles instead. Cook the noodles according to the package directions.

MUDDY EARTHWORM SPAGHETTI

Chow down on a muddy mass of worms as they navigate a plate of dirt!

Ingredients

2 15-ounce cans black beans

Sauce
2 cups barbecue sauce
1 tablespoon Worcestershire sauce
1 9-ounce jar red pepper jelly
2 tablespoons honey
2 tablespoons brown sugar
1 teaspoon red pepper flakes
1 1-pound package spaghetti

Tools

• knife
• cutting board
• medium saucepan
• measuring cups
• measuring spoons
• mixing spoon
• large stockpot
• colander
• serving plates

Serves: 4
Preparation Time: 35–40 minutes

TIP

If you don't have red pepper jelly, you can substitute seedless raspberry jam.

1. Drain the beans. Then carefully chop them into small, crumbly pieces to look like dirt.

2. Add all the sauce ingredients to a saucepan. Stir to combine. Warm the sauce on a medium-low setting for 10 to 15 minutes. Then reduce the heat to low until you are ready to use it.

3. Fill a stockpot three-quarters full with water. With an adult's help, bring the water to a boil over high heat. Add the spaghetti, and cook according to the package directions.

4. Carefully drain the spaghetti through a colander. Put the spaghetti back in the stockpot.

5. Gently stir the chopped beans into the spaghetti. Then add the sauce, and gently stir to combine.

6. Scoop the earthy mixture onto plates. Warn your guests to stab any slimy stragglers that try to escape!

1

2

5

DOG PILE ON RICE

No doo-doo bags needed for this tasty pile of chili and rice!

Ingredients

Chili

3 tablespoons olive oil

1 onion chopped into ¼-inch pieces

1 pound ground turkey

½ teaspoon dried basil

1 teaspoon ground cumin

1 teaspoon dried oregano

2 tablespoons chili powder

1 teaspoons salt

1 tablespoon of flour

1 6-ounce can of tomato paste

2 15-ounce cans chopped
    tomatoes, drained

1 15-ounce can kidney beans,
    drained

3 cups spinach leaves

Serves: 6
Preparation Time:
2–4 hours

Green Rice

½ cup cilantro

1 cup spinach leaves

1¼ cup chicken broth

1 minced garlic clove

1 teaspoon salt

2 tablespoons butter

1½ cups long-grain white rice

Tools

- measuring spoons
- large stockpot with lid
- knife
- cutting board
- mixing spoon
- blender
- medium saucepan with lid
- serving plate
- large zipper-close plastic bag
- scissors

1. To make the chili, heat 3 tablespoons of oil in a stockpot over medium heat with an adult's help. Add the chopped onion, and cook until translucent. Add the ground turkey, and cook until browned. Add the basil, cumin, oregano, chili powder, salt, flour, and tomato paste. Stir together, and cook for 5 minutes. Add the tomatoes, beans, and 3 cups of spinach leaves. Cover and simmer for 1 hour on low heat.

2

2. While the chili cooks, make the green rice. Blend cilantro, 1 cup of spinach leaves, chicken broth, 1¼ cup water, garlic, and salt in a blender.

3. Melt the butter in a saucepan over medium heat. Add the uncooked rice, and stir for 1 minute.

4. Pour the blender ingredients into the saucepan. Then turn heat up to high and bring to a boil. Turn the heat down to very low. Cover the saucepan, and cook for 30 minutes. Remove the pan from heat, keeping it covered, and set aside.

6

5. Take the chili off the heat, and let it cool. Transfer as much chili as will fit to the clean blender. Blend the chili in batches until it is smooth.

6. Scoop some of the green rice onto a serving plate. Then pour 1 cup of the chili into a plastic bag. Clip off one corner of the bag to make a hole. Squeeze a few chili droppings onto a bed of green rice. Provide guests with the proper utensils for pickup, then present your tasty poo piles!

TIP

If needed, reinforce the corner of the plastic bag with duct tape.

CREATURE-IN-MY-POT PIE

Take a bite of this creeping creature before it takes a bite out of you!

Ingredients

3 pounds boneless, skinless chicken pieces

6 tablespoons butter

salt

pepper

1 large onion

3 carrots

3 celery stalks

½ cup all-purpose flour

2½ cups chicken stock

1½ cups milk

1 teaspoon dried thyme leaves

¾ cup green peas, frozen or fresh

2 teaspoons dried parsley

2 8-ounce tubes refrigerated crescent roll dough

pimientos and almond slices (optional for decorating)

Tools

• large zipper-close plastic bag

• rolling pin

• measuring spoons

• frying pan

• tongs

• knife

• cutting board

• large stockpot

• measuring cups

• mixing spoon

• whisk

• pizza cutter

• 4 oven-safe bowls and plates

• ladle

• 1–2 baking sheets

• oven mitts

Serves: 4
Preparation Time: 1 hour, 30 minutes

1. Rinse the chicken pieces in water. Then place as many as will fit in a plastic bag. Use the rolling pin to roll the pieces out until they are the same thickness. Repeat until all the chicken is rolled out.

2. With an adult's help, heat 2 tablespoons of butter in a frying pan over medium-high heat. Add a few shakes of salt and pepper. Cook the chicken pieces for 5 to 8 minutes on one side. Turn the chicken over, and cook on the other side for 5 to 8 minutes. Turn over once more, and cook another 5 to 8 minutes or until done. Remove the chicken from heat, and let it cool. When cool, cut the chicken into bite-size pieces.

3. Chop the onion, carrots, and celery into ½-inch pieces on a clean cutting board.

4. In a stockpot, melt the remaining butter over medium heat. Add the onion, carrots, and celery. Then cook for 10 to 12 minutes.

5. Add the flour. Cook for 1 to 2 minutes, stirring constantly. Make sure all flour lumps disappear. Using a whisk, stir in the chicken stock. Next add the milk, and reduce the temperature to low. Simmer for 10 minutes, whisking often.

6. Add the cooked chicken pieces, thyme, peas, parsley, and ½ teaspoon each of salt and pepper. Stir to combine, and keep on low heat while you prepare the crust.

*Creature-in-My-Pot Pie
continued next page*

Fresh herbs can add fantastic flavor to any dish. Substitute any of the dried herbs for fresh ones to really impress your guests!

Creature-in-My-Pot Pie, continued

7 Preheat the oven to 325°F. Unroll the first crescent roll dough onto a large, clean cutting board. Use a pizza cutter to cut the dough into several small strips. Unroll the second dough and cut into four equal pieces. Shape these into four flattened circles to look like heads.

8 Place four oven-safe serving bowls on four oven-safe plates. Then ladle the filling into the bowls.

9 Place a dough strip inside the first bowl, and trail it down the outside to attach to the plate. Arrange several more strips around the bowl. Place a round piece of dough on top of the bowl to look like a head.

10 Repeat step 9 until all the bowls are decorated. Then put the plates on one or two baking sheets, depending on how much space you need. Bake for 12 to 15 minutes, or until lightly browned.

11 Wearing oven mitts, carefully remove the baking sheet from the oven and allow to cool for 7 to 10 minutes. If you like, make a face out of pimientos and almond slices. Then serve these creepy creatures to hungry guests. Remember to warn them that the bowls and plates will be hot!

SiCKENING SNACKS

Most kids reach for a snack as soon as they get home from school.

What is your go-to treat? Maybe you grab a handful of pretzels and wash them down with a tall glass of juice. Or maybe you nibble on some fruit. But what if those pretzels were covered in snot? Imagine that your juice was made of slime. Picture fruit full of fangs. These dishes may sound horrible. But you're actually in for a delicious treat!

From nasty booger sticks to spooky cake eyeballs, snacks that look terrible but taste terrific are tons of fun to make and serve. So scour the cupboards and get ready to make some delightfully disgusting snacks!

MUMMY CAKES

These mini mummy pizzas will put a curse on your guests' taste buds!

Ingredients

10–12 black olives
10–12 string cheese sticks
5 cherry tomatoes
10 rice cakes
¾ cup pizza sauce

Tools

- knife
- cutting board
- 2 baking sheets
- measuring cup
- measuring spoons
- oven mitts

Serves: 8–10
Preparation Time: 10–15 minutes

1 **Preheat** the oven to 350°F. Cut the olives into round slices. These will be your mummies' eyes.

2

2 Pull the string cheese apart into thin strands. Cut the cherry tomatoes in half.

3 Place the rice cakes on the baking sheets. Spread 1 tablespoon of pizza sauce on each cake.

4 Put two olive eyes on each rice cake. Add a cherry tomato mouth beneath the eyes.

4

5 Now cover each cake in cheese strands. Arrange them so they look like bandages.

6 With an adult's help, bake the cakes for 3 to 5 minutes. Remove, and let them cool. Your guests will be spooked as they bite into their mini mummies!

5

BOOGER STICKS

No tissues needed for these supersticky booger bites.

Ingredients

3 tablespoons cream cheese
3 tablespoons grated parmesan
   cheese
green food coloring
30–40 pretzel sticks

Tools

• baking sheet
• waxed paper
• measuring spoons
• microwave-safe bowl
• oven mitts
• rubber spatula

Serves: 4–6
Preparation Time: 30–45 minutes

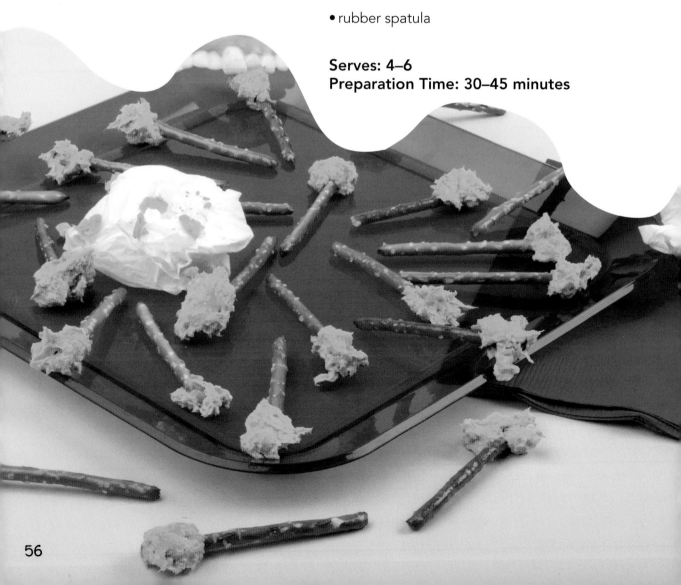

3

1 Cover a baking sheet with waxed paper.

2 Place the cream cheese in a bowl, and microwave on high for 30 seconds. Continue to heat for 15 seconds at a time, stirring between heatings, until the cream cheese is melted and gooey.

3 Carefully remove the bowl from the microwave and add the parmesan cheese. Stir the mixture together with a rubber spatula.

4

4 Stir 3 drops of food coloring into the cheese mixture. It should be a nice booger-green color. Add more food coloring if needed.

5 Dip a pretzel stick in the cheese mixture. Lift it out, and let it cool for 10 seconds. Dip the pretzel stick again, swirl it in the mixture, and lift it out again. Repeat until the cheese mixture looks like a booger on the pretzel. Then set the pretzel on the baking sheet.

6 Repeat step 5 until all the pretzel sticks are coated. Refrigerate the sticks for 10 minutes. Your boogers are ready to serve!

5

CROOKED FINGER BREAD

These twisted breadsticks look just like crooked, bloody fingers with bright-red nails!

Ingredients

cooking spray
½ red pepper
½ cup (1 stick) unsalted butter
½ teaspoon salt
1 11-ounce tube refrigerated
  breadsticks
½ cup marinara sauce

Tools

- baking sheet
- knife
- cutting board
- measuring cups
- measuring spoons
- small microwave-safe bowl
- oven mitts
- fork
- pastry brush

Serves: 5–6
Preparation Time: 30 minutes

1. Preheat the oven according to the breadsticks package instructions. Lightly coat a baking sheet with cooking spray.

2. Cut the pepper into small triangles. They should look like fingernails.

2

3. Use the microwave to melt the butter in a small bowl. Then whisk in the salt using a fork.

4. Pull the breadstick dough apart into individual breadsticks. Then twist each breadstick to look like a crooked finger. Form a big bump in the center of each breadstick to look like a knuckle. Arrange the breadsticks on the baking sheet. Then brush each breadstick lightly with the melted butter and salt mixture.

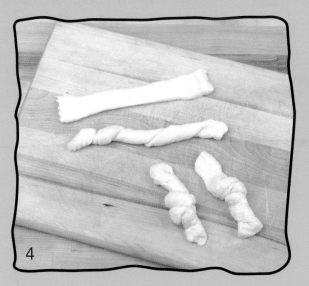
4

5. Press a pepper slice onto one tip of each breadstick to look like a fingernail.

6. With an adult's help, bake the breadsticks according to the package directions. Then remove them from the oven, and decorate your fingers with marinara sauce to look like blood. Present these bloodstained fingers to your guests, and warn them to watch out for knuckles!

5

SLIME COCKTAIL

This sewer-worthy drink may look disgusting. But it's just right for washing down salty snacks.

Ingredients

2 cups pineapple juice
2 cups white grape juice
neon green food coloring
neon blue food coloring
1 can club soda
¼ cup maple syrup

Tools

- measuring cups
- pitcher
- long-handled spoon
- shallow bowl
- mixing spoon
- 6 drinking glasses

Serves: 6
Preparation Time: 10 minutes

1. Pour the pineapple juice and grape juice into a pitcher and stir together.

2. Stir in 10 to 15 drops of neon green food coloring and 4 to 6 drops of neon blue food coloring. The liquid should be a slime-green color. Add more food coloring as needed to get the color you want.

3. Add the club soda to the pitcher, and set it aside.

4. Pour the maple syrup into a shallow bowl. Add 3 drops neon green food coloring and 1 drop of neon blue food coloring. Stir together.

5. Dip the rims of six drinking glasses in the syrup. Then fill them with the juice and soda mixture. Watch your guests try not to gag as they slurp down this tasty cocktail.

2

4

5

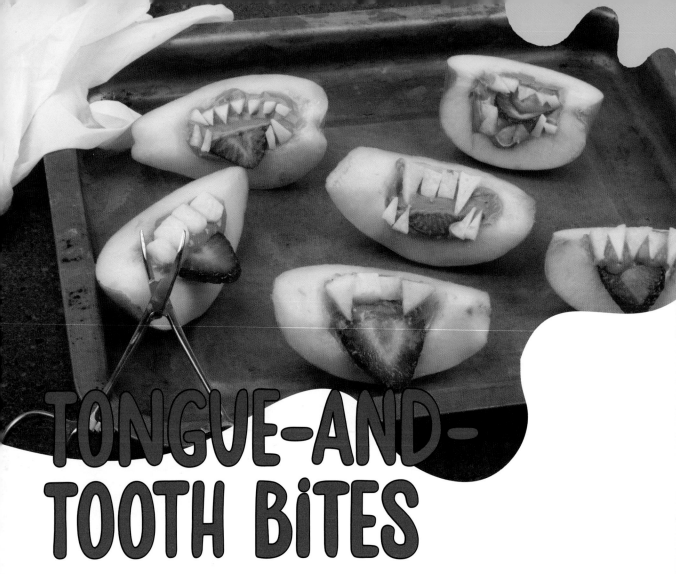

TONGUE-AND-TOOTH BITES

Chomp up these tasty bite-sized fruit pieces before they take a bite out of you!

Ingredients

2 green apples
2 pears
1 jicama
5 strawberries
⅓ cup peanut butter

Tools

- knife
- cutting board
- spoon
- peeler
- measuring cups
- table knife

Serves: 4–6
Preparation Time: 15–20 minutes

1. Cut the apples and pears into quarters. Cut the core and seeds out of each fruit piece.

1

2. Turn each fruit piece so the skin is facing out. Use a spoon to scoop out a mouth-shaped hole.

3. Peel the jicama, and slice it into long strips with an adult's help. Then cut the strips into small, tooth-sized pieces.

4. Remove the strawberry stems. Slice each berry lengthwise into four to six pieces.

2

5. Spread peanut butter inside each fruit piece's hole.

6. Stick the jicama pieces into the peanut butter to look like teeth. Then add a strawberry-slice tongue to each piece of fruit. Your toothy fruit bites are ready for snacking!

3

TIP

If one of your guests has a peanut allergy, use sunflower butter instead of peanut butter. This creamy spread is made from sunflower seeds.

CHARRED ZOMBIE-SKIN CRISPS

Crispy zombie skin makes a healthful treat.

Ingredients

Barbecue Sauce
1 cup ketchup
¼ cup apple cider vinegar
1 tablespoon honey
1 tablespoon brown sugar
1¼ teaspoons paprika
1¼ teaspoons garlic powder
1 tablespoon Worcestershire sauce
2 bunches kale

Tools

- measuring cups
- measuring spoons
- saucepan
- mixing spoon
- baking sheet
- parchment paper
- dish towel or paper towel
- knife
- cutting board
- pastry brush
- oven mitts
- tongs
- small bowl for serving

Serves: 4–6
Preparation Time: 1½ hours

1. Stir the barbecue sauce ingredients together in a saucepan. With an adult's help, bring the sauce to a simmer over medium heat. Then turn the heat to low and cook for 1 hour, stirring every 10 minutes. Remove the sauce from heat and set aside.

1

2. Preheat the oven to 350°F. Cover a baking sheet with parchment paper.

3. Wash the kale and pat it dry with a dish towel or paper towel. Cut out the stems, and chop the leaves into smaller pieces.

4. Spread out the kale leaves on the baking sheet. Brush each leaf with a small amount of barbecue sauce.

3

5. Bake the kale for 10 minutes. Use tongs to turn the leaves over and bake for another 10 to 15 minutes.

6. Remove the baking sheet from the oven, and serve the kale with a small bowl of barbecue sauce. These crispy greens may look undead, but they will be gone before you know it!

TIP

Speed up this recipe by using premade barbecue sauce.

4

POPPED BRAINS

These brains are oh-so-sweet and extra crunchy for a mind-bending treat!

Ingredients

5 tablespoons butter
1 10.5-ounce package
    marshmallows
1 tablespoon vanilla extract
red food coloring
¼ cup chopped walnuts
6–8 cups popped and lightly salted
    popcorn
½ cup white chocolate chips
¼ cup raspberry jam

Tools

• measuring spoons
• large stockpot
• baking sheet
• waxed paper
• measuring cups
• mixing spoon
• table knife

Serves: 8
Preparation Time: 15–20 minutes

1. Melt the butter in a stockpot over low heat. Cover a baking sheet with waxed paper.

2. Add the marshmallows to the stockpot, and stir until they melt. Then add the vanilla extract and 3 drops of food coloring.

3. Stir in the walnuts. Then pour in the popcorn, and stir until it is coated with the marshmallow mixture. Stir in the white chocolate chips until they melt. Remove the stockpot from heat, and allow the mixture to cool until it is safe to work with but still warm.

3

4. With clean hands, form the popcorn mixture into eight balls of equal size. Place them on the baking sheet.

5. Next gently form each ball into a brain shape. Make a slight dent down the center of each ball to look like a brain.

5

6. Use a table knife to put a line of raspberry jam down each brain's dent. These brainy bites are ready to make your snackers smarter!

TIP

Latex-free gloves can help keep your hands clean while forming these sticky brains.

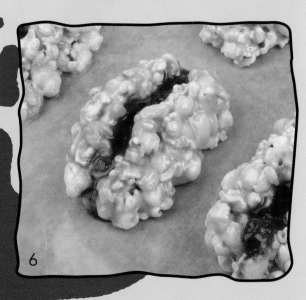

6

MUMMY DOGS

These spooky little mummies look like they came straight out of the tomb!

Ingredients

2 tablespoons mayonnaise

1 teaspoon mustard

2 black olives

1 11-ounce package refrigerated breadstick dough

8 hot dogs

ketchup, for serving

Tools

• measuring spoons

• small bowl

• mixing spoon

• knife

• cutting board

• baking sheet

• oven mitts

• toothpick

Serves: 6–8
Preparation Time: 25 minutes

1. Preheat the oven to 375°F. Stir together the mayonnaise and mustard in a small bowl. Chop the olives into tiny pieces. These will be your mummies' eyes.

2. Remove the breadstick dough from the package and pull apart into individual breadsticks. Stretch out each breadstick with your hands until it is long and skinny.

3. Wrap each hot dog in one piece of breadstick dough. The dough should look like a mummy's bandages. Arrange the dough-wrapped hot dogs on the baking sheet. Bake for 15 to 18 minutes, or until golden brown.

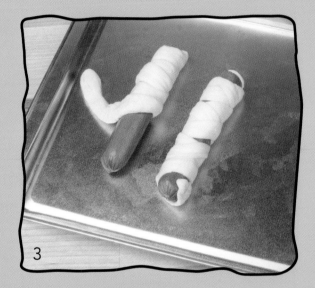

4. Remove the baking sheet from the oven, and let the hot dogs cool. Use a toothpick to add two drops of the mayonnaise-mustard mixture to each hot dog. These should look like eyes. Then add an olive-piece pupil to each drop.

5. Serve your mini mummies with a bit of ketchup to satisfy hungry snackers!

TIP

These monstrous mummies can also be made from turkey dogs or vegetarian hot dogs!

SWEET CAKE EYEBALLS

These supersweet eyeballs make a perfect snack to stare right back.

Ingredients

Cake
cooking spray
1 16.5-ounce box red velvet cake mix
⅓ cup vegetable oil (or amount on cake mix package)
3 large eggs (or amount on cake mix package)

Frosting
½ cup (1 stick) butter, softened
1 8-ounce package cream cheese
1 tablespoon vanilla extract
4 cups powdered sugar

Candy Coating
2 16-ounce packages white chocolate candy coating
20–30 small round coated chocolate candy pieces
red and black writing gel

Tools

- 1 13 x 9-inch cake pan
- measuring spoons
- measuring cups
- mixing bowls
- mixing spoons
- oven mitts
- wire cooling rack
- mixer or hand mixer
- 2 baking sheets
- waxed paper
- toothpick
- serving plate

Serves: 10–20
Preparation Time: 4–5 hours

1. Preheat the oven according to the cake mix package instructions. Lightly coat the cake pan with cooking spray.

2. Stir the cake ingredients together in a mixing bowls. Pour the batter into the cake pan, and bake according to the package instructions. Turn the cake out onto a wire rack to cool.

3

3. While the cake is cooling, make the frosting. Put the butter, cream cheese, and vanilla in a mixing bowl. Beat with a mixer on low speed. Add the powdered sugar 1 cup at a time, and beat until creamy.

4. Cover two baking sheets with waxed paper.

5. With clean hands, crumble the cake into a large bowl. Add 2 cups of frosting. Mix together with your hands.

5

6. With clean hands, form small round balls from the cake and frosting mixture. Each should be about the size of a golf ball. Put the cake balls on the baking sheet. Refrigerate them for 2 hours.

6

To tell if your cake is done cooking, insert a toothpick or table knife into the cake's center. If the toothpick or knife comes out clean, the cake is fully cooked!

Sweet Cake Eyeballs continued next page

TIP

Writing gel is a type of frosting that is perfect for creating piping or writing on desserts. It is available at most grocery stores or online.

7 When your cake balls are chilled, it's time to make the coating. Microwave the white chocolate candy coating on low power for 1 minute. Stir the coating for a few seconds. Then microwave for 30 more seconds, and stir again. Continue cooking for 30 seconds and stirring until the coating is melted.

8

8 Gently drop a cake ball in the candy coating. Use a spoon to roll the ball around in the coating until it is completely covered.

9 Place the coated cake ball back on the baking sheet. Press a candy piece in the center of the ball. The cake ball should look like an eyeball with an iris.

10 Repeat steps 8 and 9 with the remaining cake balls. Then refrigerate them for 15 more minutes.

10

11 Use the red writing gel to add veins to each eyeball.

12 Put a black dot of the writing gel in the center of each candy piece to look like a pupil. Arrange these spooky snacks on a serving plate, where they can glare at hungry guests!

11

73

DREADFUL DINNERS

What is your favorite dinner?

Perhaps stuffed peppers are your pick. Or maybe it's gooey macaroni and cheese. But what if those peppers oozed puke all over your plate? Would you eat mac and cheese if it had flakes of crusty monster skin mixed in? The answer is yes, if your dish was as tasty as it was terrifying!

Revolting dinners are tons of fun to make, serve, and eat. From meatloaf with onion fingernails to dumplings that look like dissected brains, getting grossed out at dinnertime is just plain fun. Put on your apron, and prepare to horrify hungry friends and family members with these disgusting and delicious dinners!

ZOMBIE-GUT CHILI

Oozing zombie entrails and blood clots are what's for dinner!

Ingredients

1 14-ounce package bratwurst

2 15-ounce cans great northern beans, drained

2 15-ounce cans chicken broth

2 cans whole peeled tomatoes, including the juice

2 cloves minced garlic

1 teaspoon oregano

1 teaspoon cumin

1 teaspoon chili powder

1 4-ounce can green chilies

½ teaspoon salt

1 teaspoon pepper

sour cream

food coloring in several colors

Tools

- measuring spoons
- slow cooker
- mixing spoons
- knife
- cutting board
- small bowls
- serving bowls

Serves: 6
Preparation Time: 3½–8½ hours (30 minutes active)

1. Put all the ingredients except the sour cream and food coloring in the slow cooker.

1

2. Turn the slow cooker to the low setting, and cook for 7 to 8 hours. Or cook on high for 3 to 4 hours.

3. Stir everything together with a big spoon.

4. Carefully remove the bratwurst, and chop it into sections. Then put it back in the slow cooker for 15 more minutes.

4

5. Put several spoonfuls of sour cream in each small bowl. Add several drops of food coloring to each bowl and stir in. For an extra-gross look, combine two colors, but don't mix completely. This create swirls.

6. Scoop the chili into serving bowls. Garnish with the sour cream, and enjoy some zombie-gut ooze.

5

TIP

If you don't have a slow cooker, you can make this chili using a large stockpot on the stove. Bring all ingredients to a boil, and simmer for 1 hour.

SLIMY WITCHES' HAIR SPAGHETTI

Twirl this greasy tangle of witches' hair and tomato scabs on your fork!

Ingredients

1 pound angel-hair pasta
½ cup plus 1 tablespoon olive oil
4 cloves minced garlic
1 teaspoon Italian seasoning blend
1 tablespoon dried basil
1 14½-ounce can diced tomatoes
¼ teaspoon salt
¼ teaspoon pepper
4 tablespoons grated Parmesan cheese

Tools

• large stockpot
• colander
• measuring spoons
• small glass
• large bowl
• food coloring in several colors
• mixing spoons
• serving plates

Serves: 4
Preparation Time: 1 hour

1. Fill the stockpot three-quarters full with water. With an adult's help, bring the water to a boil over medium-high heat. Add the pasta, and cook according to the package directions.

2. When the pasta is done, put 3 tablespoons of pasta water in a small glass. You will use this water later! With an adult's help, drain the pasta using a colander.

3

3. Fill a large bowl halfway with water. Add several drops of each color of food coloring to dye the water black. Then soak the pasta in the water for 15 to 20 minutes. Drain the pasta one more time, and mix with ½ cup olive oil.

4. In the clean stockpot, heat the remaining oil over medium heat. Add the garlic, and cook about 1 minute.

5. Add the Italian seasoning, basil, and tomatoes to the oil and garlic mix. Then add the salt and pepper, and cook for 5 minutes.

5

6. Add the pasta and pasta water to the pot. Then stir together for 1 minute until heated through. Swirl pasta on each plate, and garnish each serving with 1 tablespoon Parmesan cheese. Now serve up your slimy hair!

6

PUKING PEPPERS

Bake pepper people who puke up a gross-looking mix of cheesy ground beef!

Ingredients

1 pound ground beef
1 14½-ounce can diced tomatoes
½ 14½-ounce can corn
½ 14½-ounce can pinto beans
½ teaspoon salt
¼ teaspoon pepper
1 teaspoon chili powder
½ teaspoon onion powder
½ teaspoon garlic powder
3–4 bell peppers
¾ cup shredded cheese

Tools

- frying pan
- mixing spoons
- measuring spoons
- knife
- cutting board
- baking pan
- oven mitts
- serving plates

Serves: 4
Preparation Time: 45 minutes

1. Preheat the oven to 350°F. Brown the ground beef in the pan, stirring constantly. Add the tomatoes, corn, beans, salt, pepper, chili powder, onion powder, and garlic powder. Mix well, and remove the pan from heat.

2. Have an adult help you cut off each pepper's top. Set the tops aside. Then scoop out each pepper's innards and discard. Make two small slits in each pepper for eyes. Then cut one longer slit for a mouth.

3. Stand each pepper upright on the baking pan. Spoon the ground beef mixture into each one. Sprinkle cheese on top, and then replace the peppers' tops.

4. Bake the peppers for 15 to 20 minutes. Remove from oven, and plate each pepper.

5. Have an adult help you cut each eye slit to make it wider. Then cut each mouth slit from the corners all the way down to the plate. Pull the mouths open, and watch the "puke" ooze out. Your sickly peppers are ready to serve!

INTESTINE CALZONE

Cook up a slimy coil of oozing intestines!

Ingredients

1 13.8-ounce package ready-made pizza
    dough
¾ cup shredded Monterey Jack cheese
½ onion
1 8-ounce can black olives
1 24-ounce jar pizza or pasta sauce

Tools

• rolling pin
• baking sheet
• measuring cups
• knife
• cutting board
• spoon
• oven mitts

Serves: 4
Preparation Time: 45 minutes

1. Preheat the oven to the recommended temperature on the pizza dough package.

2. Roll out the dough into a large rectangle on a baking sheet.

3

3. Sprinkle the cheese over the dough. Chop the onion and olives, and sprinkle on top of the cheese. Then add about half of the sauce, and set the rest aside.

4. Carefully roll the dough into a log with the toppings inside. Pinch the log's ends together.

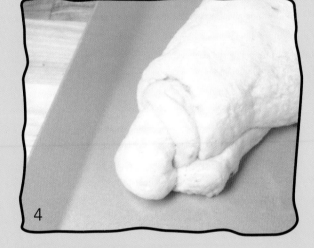

4

5. Place the log on the baking sheet. Arrange the log so it makes a zigzag shape. It should look like an intestine! Bake the pizza dough according to the package directions.

6. Remove from the oven, and add the remaining tomato sauce along the calzone's edges. It should look like gooey, oozing blood! Yum!

5

TIP

Add bits of Italian sausage or bacon to the filling for a fleshier flavor!

MONSTER-SKIN MAC AND CHEESE

An ooey, gooey pasta packed full of peeling, oozing monster skin. Watch out for warts!

Ingredients

½ cup (1 stick) butter

⅔ cup flour

2 cups whole milk

¼ teaspoon salt

½ teaspoon pepper

3 cups shredded cheddar cheese

1 cup shredded Parmesan cheese, plus a little extra for garnish

1 pound elbow pasta

8 ounces cubed smoked ham

cooking spray

4 slices cooked and chopped bacon

capers or green peas

Tools

• measuring cups

• large saucepan

• mixing spoons

• measuring spoons

• whisk

• large stockpot

• colander

• large baking dish

• oven mitts

Serves: 4
Preparation Time: 45 minutes

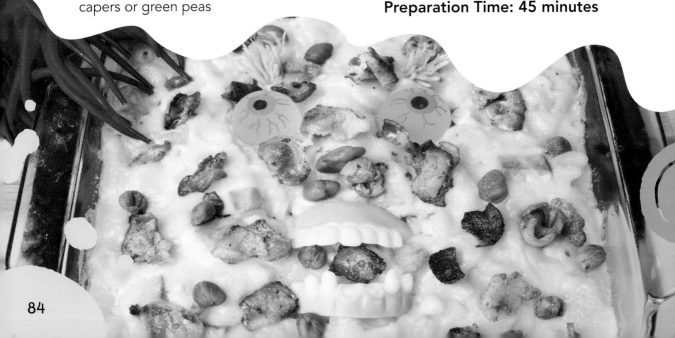

1. Preheat the oven to 350°F. Melt the butter in the bottom of a large saucepan over medium heat. Add the flour, and stir for 3 minutes over low heat.

2. Turn the heat up to medium, and add the milk. Cook until thickened, about 5 to 8 minutes. Add the salt and pepper.

3. Turn off the heat, and whisk in the cheddar cheese. Then add 1 cup of Parmesan cheese. This makes a sauce.

4. Cook the pasta in a stockpot according to the package directions. With an adult's help, drain the pasta using a colander. Then combine the pasta, cheese sauce, and ham in the stockpot, and mix together.

5. Coat the baking dish with cooking spray, and pour in the pasta mixture.

6. Sprinkle the pasta with bacon and extra Parmesan cheese. Bake for 25 to 30 minutes. When your monstrous mac and cheese is done, add caper or green pea warts for some ferocious flair!

TIP

Add Weenie Witch Fingers from page 126 for an extra gross garnish.

MAGGOT BURGERS

Make burgers swarming with squirming maggots. Eat up before they hatch!

Ingredients

1 cup uncooked rice
1 pound ground turkey or beef

Burger Seasoning
¼ teaspoon salt
1½ teaspoons paprika
1½ teaspoons garlic powder
¼ teaspoon cumin
1 teaspoon ground black pepper
¾ teaspoon dried basil
¾ teaspoon dried parsley
¼ teaspoon chili powder
½ teaspoon onion powder
4 slices white cheddar cheese
4 hamburger buns
ketchup for serving

Tools

• medium saucepan
• measuring cups
• baking dish
• measuring spoons
• mixing bowls
• mixing spoon
• broiling pan
• oven mitts
• spatula
• fork

Serves: 4
Preparation Time: 30 minutes

1. Cook the rice in the saucepan according to the package instructions. Put ½ cup of cooked rice into a small bowl. Put the rest of the rice into a baking dish. Then preheat the oven to the broil setting for 5 to 10 minutes.

2

2. Mix together the burger seasoning ingredients in a small bowl. Then mix the ground meat with the seasoning, and form four patties using clean hands.

3. Roll each patty through the rice in the baking dish. The rice should stick to the patty in some places but not everywhere.

3

4. Gently place the patties in the broiling pan, and place it in the oven. Cook for 6 to 7 minutes.

5. Remove the pan from the oven. Then flip the patties, and broil another 1 to 2 minutes.

6. Place a slice of cheese on each bun bottom, then add the patties. Pierce the patties with a fork to let some juices ooze out. Then add a little more rice from the bowl you set aside in step 1. Add the bun tops, and serve the burgers with ketchup. Can you see your maggots wiggling?

6

BACON-WRAPPED WORM

Cut into this massive meat worm before it takes a bite out of you!

Ingredients

1 1-pound pork tenderloin
8–10 bacon slices
1 apple
2 pearl onions, peeled
pimientos
greens or tomato sauce for serving

Serves: 4
Preparation Time: 4–5 hours
(30 minutes active)

Tools

- cutting board
- plastic wrap
- baking dish
- oven mitts
- tongs
- meat thermometer
- knife
- toothpicks

1. Lay the pork tenderloin on a piece of plastic wrap. Cover the pork with strips of bacon. The strips should overlap one another, so they completely cover the tenderloin. This is your worm's body.

2. Wrap the pork and bacon in plastic wrap. Place in the freezer for 3 hours. (Bacon cooks faster than tenderloin. Freezing first evens out the cooking time.)

1

3. Remove the pork from the freezer, take off the plastic wrap, and place in a baking dish. Preheat the oven as needed, then bake your worm according to the instructions on the tenderloin package.

4. Use tongs to flip the worm over. Then bake for 10 more minutes, and check for doneness.

5. Remove the pork from the oven, and allow to cool. Then, with an adult's help, cut out the worm's mouth. Add an apple slice for a spooky smile. Use toothpicks to attach onion eyes with pimiento pupils.

2

6. Serve the worm on a bed of greens or in a puddle of tomato sauce. Disgusting!

TIP

5

Use a meat thermometer to check if your pork is done. Pork is cooked when it is between 145° and 160°F. Undercooked meat can make people sick, so have an adult help make sure your worm is fully cooked!

MONSTER-HAND MEAT LOAF

A scrumptious severed hand made of meat, complete with frightening onion fingernails.

Ingredients

1½ pounds ground beef
1 egg
1 chopped onion
1 cup milk
1 cup dried bread crumbs
1 cup grated carrot
1 cup chopped spinach
¼ cup brown sugar
ketchup
¼ cup shredded cheese

Tools

- knife
- cutting board
- measuring cups
- grater
- large bowl
- large baking pan
- oven mitts
- meat thermometer

Serves: 4
Preparation Time: 1 hour, 20 minutes

1. Preheat the oven to 350°F. Put all the ingredients except the ketchup and shredded cheese in a large bowl. Save a handful of onion slices for later. Mix together the ingredients with clean hands.

1

2. In a large baking pan, form a hand with the meat mixture. Shape a large palm and wrist. Then form the fingers.

3. Place a slice of onion on the end of each finger to look like a fingernail.

4. Bake the hand for 40 minutes. Take the meat loaf out. Then decorate with ketchup and cheese to make it look like a supergross hand. Bake another 10 minutes, and check for doneness.

5. Place meat loaf hand on a serving dish, and add more ketchup. Then serve this horrifying hand to unsuspecting diners!

3

TIP

Ground beef is safe to eat at 160°F. Use a meat thermometer to make sure your monster hand is done.

4

BRAIN-CHUNK DUMPLINGS

What do diners think of squiggly brain bits? Find out as your guests dine on these delicious dumplings!

Ingredients

Dumpling and Filling

8 ounces white mushrooms
2 baby bok choy
2 carrots
6 green onions
3 tablespoons grapeseed oil
3 cloves minced garlic
3 tablespoons freshly grated ginger
¼ cup soy sauce
2 tablespoons ketchup
¼ teaspoon salt
1 14-ounce package wonton wrappers
2 tablespoons cornstarch

Sauce

1 cup soy sauce
1 cup ketchup
¼ cup grapeseed oil
4 teaspoons freshly grated ginger

Tools

- knife
- cutting board
- large frying pan
- measuring spoons
- mixing spoons
- grater
- measuring cups
- mixing bowls
- baking sheet
- waxed paper
- whisk
- pastry brush
- paper towels
- 2 aluminum pie tins
- rolling pin
- screwdriver or scissors
- stockpot or saucepan
- 4–5 binder clips
- serving bowls

Serves: 4
Preparation Time: 1 hour

1. Chop the mushrooms, bok choy, carrots, and green onions into ¼ to ½-inch pieces.

2. With an adult's help, heat the oil in the frying pan over medium heat. Add the mushrooms, bok choy, carrots, and green onions. Cook for 5 to 7 minutes, stirring regularly.

3. Add the garlic, ginger, soy sauce, and ketchup, and cook for another 3 minutes. The liquid will begin to evaporate. Add the salt. Put all the cooked ingredients into a bowl. Then refrigerate for 20 minutes.

4. Line the baking sheet with a piece of waxed paper. Whisk together the cornstarch and 1 cup water.

5. Place two stacked wonton wrappers on the baking sheet. Brush the cornstarch mixture onto the top wrapper. Put a heaping teaspoon of filling in the middle. Fold the wrappers into a triangle and seal the edges. Trim the edge about ¼ inch from the filling pocket. This is your first brain!

6. Cover your first brain with a damp paper towel while you stuff more brains. Repeat steps 5 and 6 until you run out of wrappers or filling.

Brain-Chunk Dumplings continued next page

TIP

For a meaty meal, try mixing the veggie filling with 1 pound of ground pork or turkey.

Brain-Chunk Dumplings, continued

7 Now make a steamer with the pie tins. Poke sixteen to twenty holes in the bottom of each tin with a clean screwdriver or scissors. Be careful not to cut yourself on the holes' sharp edges. Next flatten one tin with a rolling pin.

7

8 Add about 2 inches of water to a stockpot, and bring to a boil over medium-high heat. With an adult's help, place the unflattened pie tin over the pot's opening. Add five to six wonton brains to the tin. Then place the flattened tin on top of the first tin.

8

9 With adult help, secure the tins' edges with binder clips. Be careful—the steam will be hot! Cook for 5 to 6 minutes. Repeat until all of the brains are cooked.

10 Stir the sauce ingredients together in a bowl. Then toss each brain in the sauce to coat it.

11 Divide your dumplings into serving bowls. Now sit back and watch your guests enjoy these dumpling brains!

10

DISGUSTING DESSERTS

Imagine digging a fork into freshly baked cake covered in creamy frosting. Picture biting into an apple with an ooey-gooey candy coating, or snacking on a big bowl of jiggly gelatin. Sounds sweet, right? Now imagine that cake is smothered in blood instead of frosting. Or the apple is coated in tar, and the gelatin looks like slimy snot. Would you still eat these treats? Yes, if you knew how great they would taste!

From a cake that looks like it is topped with cat droppings to cereal treats that look like raw meat, revolting desserts are tons of fun. So roll up your sleeves and prepare to make sickening desserts that are super sweet!

MEAT TREATS

These tasty treats look like they came straight from the butcher's shop.

Serves: 4
Preparation Time: 10–30 minutes

Ingredients

3 tablespoons butter
1 10-ounce bag mini marshmallows
1 teaspoon vanilla extract
several drops red food coloring
6 cups crispy rice cereal
¾ cup strawberry or raspberry jam

Tools

- large stockpot
- measuring spoons
- measuring cups
- rubber spatula or mixing spoon
- 13 x 9-inch baking pan
- waxed paper
- knife

1. With an adult's help, melt the butter in the stockpot over low heat. Add the marshmallows, and cook until melted and smooth, stirring constantly.

2. Add the vanilla extract and food coloring. Stir together until the mixture is a light red color.

3

3. Remove the pot from heat. Stir in the cereal until all pieces are coated in the marshmallow mixture. Add the jam and stir some more.

4. Cover the bottom and sides of a baking pan with waxed paper. Pour the cereal mixture into the pan.

4

5. Cover the cereal with another sheet of waxed paper and press down firmly until the cereal is packed and even. Allow it to cool for 10 to 15 minutes.

6. Cut the cereal into squares, then gently shape each square into a patty, so it looks like a raw hamburger. Now watch your diners gobble up your sweet meat treats!

6

BIG OL' BOWL OF SNOT

What's green and slimy and very sweet?
A bowl of mucus, of course!

Serves: 4
Preparation Time: 4 hours
(1 hour active)

Ingredients

4 bananas
1 6-ounce package instant lime gelatin
½ cup small pineapple chunks
½ cup raisins

Tools

- mixing bowls
- fork
- measuring cups
- mixing spoon
- serving bowls

1

1 Put the bananas in a large bowl and mash them with a fork. Add 1 cup of hot water and stir together.

2 In another large bowl, make the lime gelatin according to the package instructions.

3 Add the banana mixture to the gelatin. Stir in the pineapple chunks and raisins.

4 Put the bowl in the refrigerator, and let it chill for at least 3 hours.

5 Spoon the mixture into individual bowls, and your snot is ready to slurp up!

2

3

POISONED ROTTEN APPLE

This tempting fruit looks good enough to eat—if you dare.

Serves: 4
Preparation Time: 1 hour
(30 minutes active)

Ingredients

4 apples
1 12-ounce package of semi-sweet
   chocolate chips
¼ teaspoon salt
1 teaspoon black gel food coloring

Tools

- baking sheet
- parchment paper
- plate
- 4 clean wooden craft sticks
- small saucepan
- rubber spatula
- measuring spoons

1. Cover a baking sheet with parchment paper and set aside. Wash and dry the apples. Remove the apple stems. Place the apples upside down on a plate. Hold an apple with one hand, and push a craft stick into the center. Push it in about three-quarters of the way, rotating gently as you go. Repeat with the remaining apples.

1

2. Put the chocolate chips in the saucepan. With an adult's help, melt the chips over low heat, stirring constantly. Once the chips are melted, stir in the salt.

3. Remove the pan from the heat, and add several drops of food coloring. Stir the chocolate sauce until it is very dark, adding more food coloring if needed.

4

4. Hold an apple by the stick. Swirl it in the chocolate until the sides of the apple are coated in sauce.

5. Hold the apple above the pan to let any excess chocolate drip off. Then carefully set it on the prepared baking sheet.

6. Repeat steps 4 and 5 with the remaining apples. Then refrigerate them for 30 minutes. Watch your guests cringe as they take a bite out of these deadly-looking but delicious treats.

5

USED BANDAGE DELIGHTS

Gross out your family and friends with these bloody bandage treats.

Serves: 6–8
Preparation Time: 10 minutes

Ingredients

4 graham crackers
8 mini marshmallows
2 tablespoons raspberry jam

Tools

- knife
- cutting board
- microwave-safe plate
- measuring spoons
- table knife
- serving plate

1. Carefully cut or break apart the graham crackers along the seams.

2. Cut each marshmallow in half.

3. Place the graham crackers on a microwave-safe plate. Place a marshmallow slice in the middle of each cracker.

4. Spread a small amount of jam on top of each marshmallow.

5. Heat the graham crackers and marshmallows in the microwave for 30 seconds. The marshmallows should just begin to ooze.

6. Arrange your bandages on a serving plate, and let these gag-worthy snacks disgust your diners!

CAT LITTER CAKE

This cat poo cake will have guests meowing for seconds.

Serves: 10
Preparation Time: 1½ hours (30 minutes active)

Ingredients

Cakes

1 16.5-ounce chocolate cake mix

⅓ cup oil (or amount on cake mix package)

3 large eggs (or amount on cake mix package)

1 16.5-ounce yellow cake mix

⅓ cup oil (or amount on cake mix package)

3 large eggs (or amount on cake mix package)

Pudding

1 5.1-ounce package vanilla instant pudding mix

2 cups cold milk (or amount on pudding package)

15–20 white sandwich cookies

12 small Tootsie Rolls, unwrapped

Tools

• mixing bowls
• measuring cups
• measuring spoons
• mixing spoon
• 2 13 x 9-inch baking pans
• oven mitts
• whisk
• blender
• microwave-safe bowl
• serving dish or bowl

1. Preheat the oven to the temperature on the cake mix packages. Make both cakes according to the package directions. When they are done baking, let the cakes cool.

1

2. Whisk together the pudding mix and milk in a bowl. Then chill the pudding in the refrigerator for 10 minutes or until the pudding is thick.

3. Put two handfuls of cookies in a blender, and blend on the low setting until the cookies are crumbled.

4. Crumble the cakes into a large bowl. Add in half of the crumbled cookies. Mix in the pudding a few tablespoons at a time until all the crumbs are combined. You may not need all the pudding.

3

5. Put the Tootsie Rolls in a microwave-safe bowl. Microwave them on high for 15 seconds at a time. Stop when the rolls are easy to bend, but not completely melted. Then shape the Tootsie Rolls into poo-shaped pieces. Be careful! The Tootsie Rolls may be hot.

6. Transfer the cake mixture to a serving dish or bowl. Arrange the Tootsie Rolls in and on top of the cake. The sight of this crumbly cake may make some guests gag, but the taste will leave them wanting more!

4

To check if a cake is done, slide a toothpick or clean table knife into it. If the knife or toothpick comes out clean, your cake is fully cooked.

SWEET WORMS IN DIRT

Creepy-crawly worms buried in cookie dirt make a perfect wriggly snack.

Serves: 6–8
Preparation Time: 5½ hours
(30 minutes active)

Ingredients

2 6-ounce packages instant
    raspberry gelatin
3 packets unflavored gelatin
    powder
1 cup whipping cream
15 drops green food coloring
30–40 chocolate sandwich cookies

Tools

- measuring cups
- saucepan
- large mixing bowl
- mixing spoons or spatulas
- 1 large package bendable straws
- tall, narrow container with a flat
    bottom, such as a vase
- cup with a spout
- rolling pin
- baking sheet
- large plastic bag
- serving bowl or plate

108

1 With an adult's help, boil 2¾ cups water in a saucepan over medium-high heat. Pour the hot water into a mixing bowl. Then stir in the raspberry and unflavored gelatin.

2 Let the mixture cool for 20 minutes or until it is lukewarm. Then mix in the whipping cream and green food coloring.

2

3 Arrange the straws in the container so the straws' ends are flush with the bottom. Pack the container very tightly so it is completely full. Carefully pour the gelatin mixture into the straws, filling them all the way to the top. Refrigerate the container for 4 hours, until the gelatin is firm.

4 Using a rolling pin, roll over the straws to loosen the gelatin worms. Then use your fingers to carefully squeeze the worms out onto a baking sheet. Refrigerate for another hour.

3

5 Seal the cookies in a large plastic bag. Crush the cookies by rolling them with a rolling pin. The cookies will be your dirt!

6 Organize the worms on a serving bowl or plate, and cover them with cookie dirt. Pull some worms halfway out, and let others wiggle on top. Warn your guests to watch their worms so they don't wriggle away!

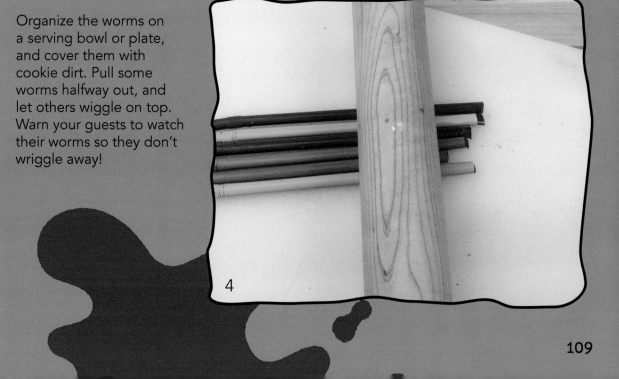

4

BLOOD SUCKERS

This gruesome dessert is the perfect on-the-go treat for vampire-loving friends and family.

Serves: 10–12
Preparation Time: 30–45 minutes

Ingredients

10–15 maraschino cherries
red food coloring
2 cups granulated sugar
4 tablespoons light corn syrup

Tools

- knife
- cutting board
- small bowl
- baking sheet
- parchment paper
- 15 white lollipop sticks
- measuring cups
- measuring spoons
- small saucepan
- candy thermometer
- large bowl

1 Chop the cherries and put them in a small bowl. Then mix in several drops of food coloring.

2 Cover a baking sheet with parchment paper. Space the lollipop sticks on the baking sheet about 3 inches apart. The sticks should all face the same direction.

3 With an adult's help, bring the sugar, corn syrup, and ¼ cup of water to a boil in a saucepan over medium heat. This makes a liquid candy mixture. Let the mixture boil for 5 to 7 minutes, and test the temperature with a candy thermometer. The mixture is done when it is 300° to 310°F.

3

4 Fill a large bowl with ice water. With an adult's help, place the saucepan in the bowl. Let the pan sit in the ice water for 20 to 30 seconds. Then stir the mixture for 1 minute.

4

5 Have an adult help with this step. The liquid candy is very hot! Scoop 1 tablespoon of the liquid candy on top of each lollipop stick. Once you have candy puddles around each stick, place a drop or two of cherry mixture in the center of each puddle. Then add several drops of food coloring to each puddle. The candy hardens quickly, so you will need to work fast.

5

6 Let the candy cool for 10 minutes. Then watch your guests' looks of disgust as they lick up these bloody suckers.

TIP

If you don't have a candy thermometer, scoop out ½ teaspoon of liquid candy and drop it into cold water. Then take it out right away. If it's done, the candy should separate into threads.

ALIEN LIMB

Create an alien autopsy scene that tastes amazing!

Serves: 6
Preparation Time: 2–3 hours
(30 minutes active)

Ingredients

2 6-ounce packages instant gelatin,
   any flavor
1 cup canned pears
1 cup pineapple chunks
red licorice
1 cup grapes

Tools

- newspaper
- masking tape
- aluminum foil
- baking pan
- plastic wrap
- measuring cups
- mixing bowls
- mixing spoons
- serving dish
- knife
- cutting board

1 Roll several newspaper sheets into a cone shape. Use masking tape to attach more newspaper sheets to the cone. It should begin to look like a tentacle. Keep adding newspapers until the limb is the size you want. Wrap three to four pieces of foil around one half of the newspaper pages. This makes a mold.

1

2 Remove the newspaper and set the mold in the baking pan. Curve the foil if needed to fit the mold in the pan. Cover the inside of the mold with plastic wrap.

3 Mix together both batches of gelatin in separate bowls according to the packages' instructions. Pour one batch into your mold. Keep the second batch in the mixing bowl. Refrigerate both batches for 30 to 40 minutes or until firm.

2

4 Remove the mold from the refrigerator, and decorate the gelatin limb with pieces of fruit and candy. Use pear pieces and pineapple chunks for bones. Licorice could be blood vessels. Get creative!

5 Melt the second batch of gelatin in the microwave for 30 seconds at a time until it is runny. Then pour it on top of the fruit. Refrigerate the gelatin for 1 to 2 hours.

6 Remove the mold from the refrigerator. Place it upside-down in a serving dish. Carefully remove the mold from the gelatin. Then cut the grapes in half, and place them on the tentacle to look like suction cups. Your creepy alien arm is ready to serve!

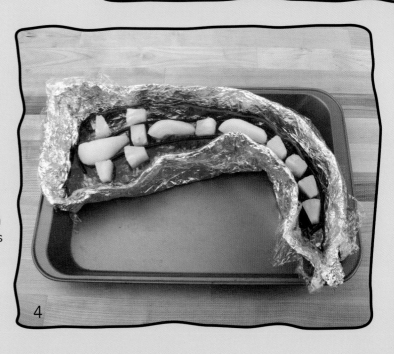

4

BLOOD-SPLATTERED CAKE

This mess of a cake makes a terrifying treat for gore-loving guests.

Serves: 4–6
Preparation Time: 1½–2 hours
(45 minutes active)

Ingredients

Cake

cooking spray
2 cups white sugar
1¾ cups all-purpose flour
¾ cup unsweetened cocoa powder
1½ teaspoons baking powder
1½ teaspoons baking soda
1 teaspoon salt
2 eggs
1 cup milk
½ cup vegetable oil
1 tablespoon vanilla extract
½ cup strawberry jam

Frosting

1 cup (2 sticks) unsalted butter,
    softened to room temperature
4 cups powdered sugar
4 tablespoons heavy whipping
    cream
2 tablespoons vanilla extract
¼ teaspoon salt

Blood-Splatter Sauce

3 tablespoons cornstarch
1 teaspoon red food coloring
1–2 drops green food coloring
1 teaspoon maple syrup

Tools

- 9-inch round cake pan
- 6-inch round cake pan
- measuring cups
- measuring spoons
- mixing bowls, various sizes
- mixing spoons
- saucepan
- mixer or hand mixer
- oven mitts
- toothpick or table knife
- wire cooling rack
- serving plate
- rubber spatula or table knife
- whisk
- newspaper
- brand-new toothbrush

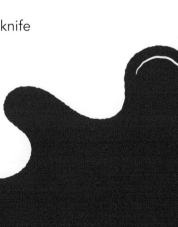

1 Preheat the oven to 350°F. Coat the cake pans with cooking spray.

2 Start by making the cake. Stir together the sugar, flour, cocoa powder, baking powder, baking soda, and salt in a large mixing bowl. With an adult's help, bring 1 cup of water to a boil over medium-high heat.

3 Form a hole in the center of the dry cake ingredients, and add the eggs, milk, oil, and vanilla to the hole. Using the mixer on medium speed, blend together all the ingredients for 3 minutes. With an adult's help, add the boiling water. Then mix until all the ingredients are combined.

4 Pour the batter into the cake pans and bake for 20 to 30 minutes or until done. Insert a toothpick or table knife into the cakes to check if they are done. If the toothpick or knife comes out clean, the cake is fully cooked. Remove the cake from the oven to cool for 10 to 15 minutes. Then flip the cakes out onto a wire rack, and cool for 1 hour.

5 While the cakes are cooling, make the frosting. Put the butter in a mixing bowl and mix it on low speed for 3 to 5 minutes. Remember to clean the mixer parts between uses. Stop when the butter is creamy and pale.

6 Add the powdered sugar, ½ cup at a time. Then mix in the heavy cream, one teaspoon at a time. If the frosting is too runny, add more powdered sugar. If it is too stiff, add more cream.

Blood-Splattered Cake continued next page

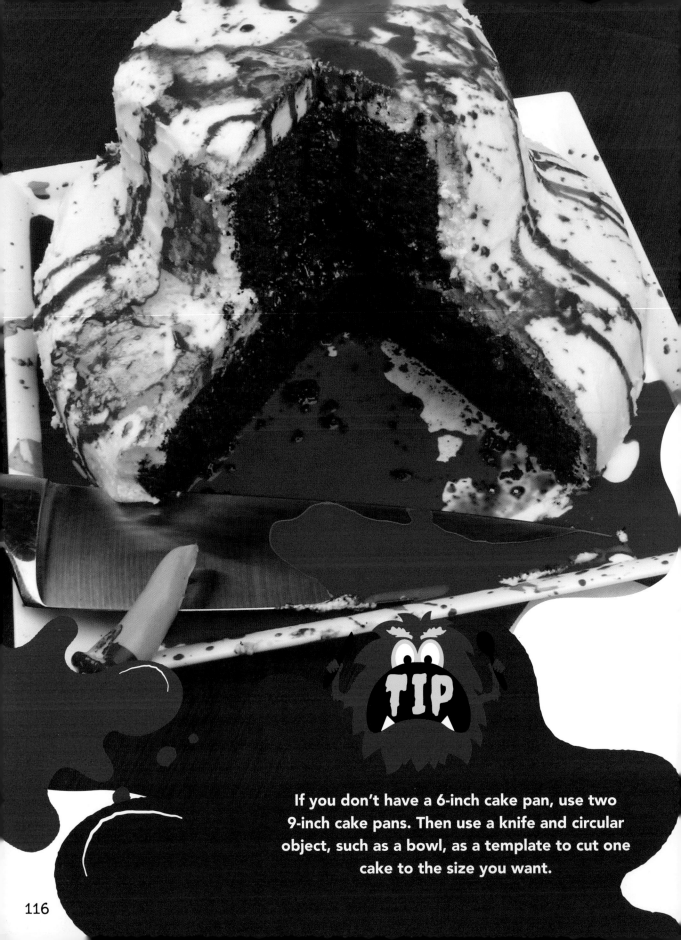

TIP

If you don't have a 6-inch cake pan, use two 9-inch cake pans. Then use a knife and circular object, such as a bowl, as a template to cut one cake to the size you want.

7 Add the vanilla and salt to the frosting mixture. Beat with the mixer on medium-high speed for 3 to 4 minutes.

8 Place the larger cake on a serving plate. Spread the jam in a circle in the center of the cake. Then set the smaller cake on top of the jam.

8

9 Use a rubber spatula or table knife to gently spread the frosting all over the cake. Be careful not to let the spatula pick up any crumbs. Then let the frosting dry for 20 to 30 minutes.

10 Next whisk all blood-splatter sauce ingredients together in a small bowl with 1 tablespoon of water.

9

11 The next step is messy, so cover your work surface with newspaper. You may even want to set up the newspaper outside if the weather is nice. Set the serving plate and cake on top of the newspaper.

12 Coat the toothbrush bristles in the sauce. Then flick the toothbrush at the cake. This should splatter the sauce all over the cake. Repeat until your cake has enough splatter. Dribble the rest of the sauce down the sides of the cake. Tell your guests to watch out for severed fingers as they dig into this disgusting dessert!

12

FOUL PARTY FOODS

Say you're at a party and scoping out the snack table. You'd probably expect to find fruity punch, crunchy chips, and towers of treats. But what if there were shrunken heads bobbing in the punch? Or blobs of brown butterscotch earwax clinging to candy sticks? Imagine a plate of chocolate cookies labeled "dog doo-doo." These snacks may seem disgusting. But you'd be in for a tasty surprise!

Revolting party foods are tons of fun to make and serve. Their sick-sounding names and appearances are just a trick. These dishes actually taste delicious! You will happily horrify your guests with party foods that look and sound gross. So put on your apron and party hat, and start making some foul eats fit for any fiesta!

EARWAX ON A STICK

Partygoers won't know whether to lick their lips or clean their ears when they see these crusty treats!

Ingredients

40–60 mini marshmallows (1 bag)
20–30 pretzel sticks
½ cup butterscotch chips

Tools

- baking sheet
- waxed paper
- microwave-safe bowl
- measuring cups
- mixing spoon

Serves: 10–15
Preparation Time:
30–45 minutes

1. Cover a baking sheet with waxed paper. Push a mini marshmallow onto each end of the pretzel sticks.

2. Put the butterscotch chips in a bowl. Microwave them for 30 seconds on high. Stir to see if the chips are melted. If not, heat the chips for another 30 seconds and stir again. Repeat until the chips are fully melted.

3. Dip the marshmallow on one end of a pretzel stick into the melted butterscotch. Then dip the other end. Place the stick on the baking sheet to cool.

4. Repeat step 3 with the remaining sticks. Now see if your guests can stomach these sweet chunks of ear gunk!

TIP

For an extra-sweet treat, add a mini chocolate chip to the end of each marshmallow after dipping it in butterscotch.

SHRUNKEN-HEAD PUNCH

Carve crisp apples into tiny bobbing heads that grimace at guests.

Ingredients

2 cups lemon juice
2 tablespoons coarse salt
8–10 Granny Smith apples
10 cups apple juice
2 cups cranberry juice
3 cups orange juice
3 cups club soda

Tools

- baking sheet
- parchment paper
- medium mixing bowl
- measuring cups
- measuring spoons
- mixing spoon
- peeler
- knife
- cutting board
- plate
- dish towel or paper towel
- oven mitts
- large punch bowl

Serves: 15
Preparation Time: 3 hours

1. Preheat the oven to 250°F. Cover a baking sheet with parchment paper. In a medium bowl, stir together the lemon juice and salt.

2

2. Peel the apples, and cut each one in half. Remove the cores and seeds. With an adult's help, carefully carve a face in the apple.

3. Cover a plate with a dish towel or paper towel. Put each apple facedown in the lemon and salt mixture for 1 minute. Remove and set each apple facedown on the plate to drain.

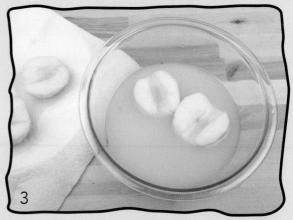

3

4. Place the apples face up on the baking sheet, and bake for 90 to 115 minutes, or until the edges begin to brown. Remove the apples from the oven, and let them cool completely.

5. Pour the apple juice, cranberry juice, orange juice, and club soda into a large punch bowl, and stir together.

6. Drop the apple heads into the punch so they glare at your guests!

4

STABBED EYEBALLS

Freshly-plucked fruit eyeballs stare at you from the other side of a toothpick.

Serves: 10–20
Preparation Time:
30–45 minutes

Ingredients

honeydew melon
½ cup strawberry jam
30–40 blueberries

Tools

- knife
- cutting board
- spoon
- melon baller
- table knife
- measuring cups
- measuring spoons
- 30–40 toothpicks
- serving platter

1. With an adult's help, cut the honeydew melon in half. Scoop out the seeds with a spoon. Use the melon baller to scoop out 30 to 40 melon balls. These will be the eyeballs.

1

2. Gently carve a hole in the middle of each melon ball using a table knife.

3. Put about ¼ teaspoon of jam in each melon ball's hole.

4. Place a blueberry on top of the jam in each melon ball.

3

5. Stick a toothpick in each eyeball for serving.

6. Arrange the eyeballs on a platter, and watch your guests pick up these fruity peepers.

TIP

If blueberries are not in season where you live, try using raisins instead.

4

WEENiE WiTCH FiNGERS

Wrinkled weenie fingers look like they came from a witch's wiggling hand!

Serves: 10–20
Preparation Time: 1 hour

Ingredients

1 14-ounce package mini cocktail
    wieners
1 white onion
½ cup ketchup

Tools

- medium saucepan
- cutting board
- knife
- colander
- measuring cups
- measuring spoons
- serving plate

1. Fill a medium saucepan three-quarters full with water. With an adult's help, bring the water to a boil over high heat. Lay the weenies out on a cutting board. Carefully cut a notch out of the tip of each weenie.

2. Cut shallow slits in the weenies to look like knuckles. Look at your own fingers for inspiration!

3. Cut the onion into thick slices. Each should be about ¾ inch wide and 1 inch long. You will need one slice for each weenie. Put the onion slices and weenies in the boiling water. Cook the weenies according to the package directions.

4. With an adult's help, drain the weenies and onion slices using a colander. Let them cool.

5. Transfer the weenies to a clean surface. Spread about ¼ teaspoon of ketchup in each weenie's notch. Place an onion slice on top of the ketchup to look like a fingernail.

6. Arrange the fingers on a serving plate, and spread the rest of the ketchup around to look like blood. Your guests won't be able to keep their hands off these fingers!

1

2

TIP

For more festive fingernails, try slices of green, yellow, or orange peppers.

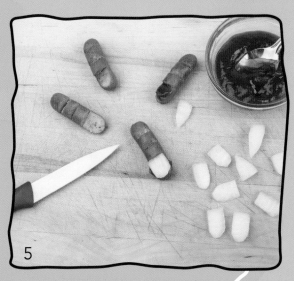

5

WITCHES' BREW

This creepy cauldron will make party guests cackle with delight.

Serves: 10–20
Preparation Time: 25 hours
(1 hour active)

Ingredients

4 cups cranberry juice
5 cups pineapple juice
1 12-ounce can frozen lemonade, thawed
½ cup lemon juice
1 bunch green grapes
8 cups ginger ale

Tools

• 2 disposable gloves
• measuring cups
• 2 rubber bands
• shallow baking dish
• punch bowl
• long-handled spoon
• kitchen scissors
• knife
cutting board

128

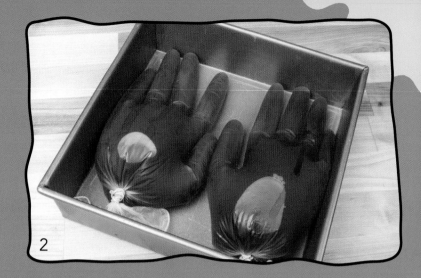

1. Wash the gloves with soap and water.

2. Carefully pour about 1½ cups of cranberry juice into each glove. Fill the gloves just past the wrist, and secure each with a rubber band. Place both gloves in a baking dish, and freeze for 24 hours.

2

3. Pour the remaining cranberry juice and the pineapple juice, lemonade, and lemon juice into a large punch bowl. Stir together.

4. Take your frozen gloves out of the freezer. Carefully cut a large slit in the palm of each glove. Gently peel the glove off the frozen hand. Be extra careful around the fingers!

4

5. Rinse the grapes, and slice each one in half. Add the grapes and ginger ale to the punch. Serve to your guests, and warn them to watch out for slimy eyeballs!

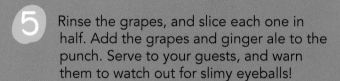

5

TIP

Many people have latex allergies, so make sure your gloves are latex-free!

DOG-PILE TREATS

Create cocoa cookies that look just like poo piles from the lawn!

Ingredients

½ cup peanut butter

¼ cup cocoa powder

1 cup milk

2 teaspoons vanilla extract

½ cup oatmeal

¾ cup brown sugar

2½ cups flour, plus extra for coating
   your hands

¼ cup raisins or chocolate chips

¼ cup raw sunflower seeds

Serves: 10–20
Preparation Time: 1 hour

Tools

• 2 baking sheets

• parchment paper

• measuring cups

• measuring spoons

• large mixing bowl

• mixing spoon

• oven mitts

• wire cooling rack

2

1 Preheat the oven to 325°F. Cover two baking sheets with parchment paper.

2 Put all the ingredients in a mixing bowl and stir together.

3 Coat your clean hands with flour. Then roll a ball of dough about the size of a golf ball.

3

4 Roll and stretch the ball into a poo shape, and place it on a baking sheet.

5 Repeat steps 3 and 4 until all the dough is used. Combine some dough chunks to form piles.

6 Bake the cookies for 20 to 25 minutes, Remove the cookies from the oven, and let them cool on a wire rack. No pooper-scooper needed for these tasty poo piles!

5

BLACK WIDOW CHEESE BALL

Use crackers to scoop up the creamy cheese guts of a supersized spider.

Serves: 10
Preparation Time: 1 hour

Ingredients

4 large shallots
3 tablespoons unsalted butter
10 ounces fresh goat cheese
10 ounces cream cheese
1 cup black sesame seeds
¼ red pepper
crackers for serving

Tools

- knife
- cutting board
- measuring spoons
- frying pan
- food processor or blender
- measuring cups
- large plate
- serving platter
- 4 black pipe cleaners
- scissors

1. Peel the shallots, and chop each one into a few small pieces. Then with an adult's help, melt the butter in a frying pan over medium-low heat. Add the shallots to the butter and sauté over medium heat for 8 to 10 minutes. Remove from heat and let the shallots cool.

2. Put the shallots, goat cheese, and cream cheese in the food processor or blender. Blend on high for 2 to 3 minutes, or until smooth. Chill in the refrigerator for 30 minutes.

3. With clean hands, roll about ⅓ of the cheese mixture into a ball. Roll the rest of the mixture into a larger ball.

4. Spread the sesame seeds out onto a large plate. Roll both cheese balls in the seeds until the balls are completely covered.

5. Arrange the balls side by side on a serving platter. They should look like the head and body of a spider. Cut four pipe cleaners in half. Stick four pipe cleaner pieces into each side of the body. They should be spaced evenly to look like legs.

6. Cut the red pepper into small pieces, and arrange them in a pattern on the spider's back. Serve this spooky spider with crackers to startle your guests!

TIP

A shallot is a type of small onion that is very sweet and mild. If you don't have shallots handy, substitute one chopped onion.

MONSTER BOOGERS

Popcorn glazed in sweet sauce becomes beastly boogers coated in snot!

Serves: 10–15
Preparation Time: 30 minutes

Ingredients

12 cups popped popcorn
12 tablespoons (1½ sticks) butter
2 cups sugar
¾ cup light corn syrup
3 tablespoons vanilla extract
green food coloring
4 cups butterscotch chips

Tools

- measuring cups
- large bowl
- baking sheet
- parchment paper
- medium saucepan
- mixing spoon
- measuring spoons

1. Put the popcorn in a large bowl. Cover a baking sheet with parchment paper.

2. With an adult's help, melt the butter in the saucepan over medium-low heat. Add the sugar, and stir for 5 to 7 minutes. Then stir in the corn syrup, vanilla extract, and several drops of food coloring.

2

3. Remove the saucepan from the heat, and carefully drizzle the sweet mixture over the popcorn. Stir until coated.

4. Let the mixture cool. Then add the butterscotch chips, and mix some more.

3

5. With clean hands, form a golf ball-sized amount of the popcorn mixture into a booger-shaped lump and place on the baking sheet. Repeat until all your boogers are made. Then place the baking sheet in the freezer for 10 minutes.

6. Remove the baking sheet from the freezer, and your boogers are ready to serve! Give guests a stack of tissues to mop up any sticky drips or massive globs.

TIP

5

With an adult's help, you can pop your own popcorn by heating 3 tablespoons of olive oil in a large stockpot over medium heat. When the oil is hot, add ½ cup unpopped kernels, and put a lid on the pot. Cook for 5 to 7 minutes, shaking the pot constantly to keep the popcorn from burning. When you hear the popping stop, remove from heat. Repeat until you have enough popcorn!

CRISPY MICE

These stuffed rodents won't squeak once they're cooked!

Serves: 10-15
Preparation Time: 2 hours (45 minutes active)

Ingredients

1 sweet onion
1 red pepper
3 cups shredded Monterey jack cheese
20–30 spaghetti strands
2 teaspoons paprika
1 teaspoon garlic powder
6 tablespoons butter, softened
10 ounces cream cheese
1½ teaspoons salt
1 teaspoon ground pepper
10–15 Anaheim peppers (or any narrow, mild peppers)
40–60 pretzel sticks
2 cups flour
2 eggs
½ cup milk
1½ cup breadcrumbs
cooking spray

Tools

- knife
- cutting board
- mixing bowls, various sizes
- measuring cups
- medium saucepan
- colander
- measuring spoons
- mixing spoons
- whisk
- baking sheets
- baking pan with grilling rack
- oven mitts
- serving plate

1. Chop the onion into ¼-inch pieces. Then chop the red pepper into ½-inch pieces. Put the onion and pepper pieces in a medium bowl, and add the Monterey jack cheese.

2. With an adult's help, fill a saucepan three-quarters full with water, and bring it to a boil over medium-high heat. Then add the spaghetti, and cook for 8 to 10 minutes, or until done. Carefully drain the spaghetti with a colander, and let it cool.

3

3. Put the paprika, garlic powder, butter, cream cheese, 1 teaspoon salt, and ½ teaspoon pepper in a large bowl. Stir together. Stir in the onion, pepper, and cheese mixture. Then refrigerate for 30 to 45 minutes.

4. Cut off the Anaheim peppers' stems. Then cut each pepper in half the long way. Use a spoon to scrape the seeds off each pepper's interior. Discard the seeds.

4

5. Lay the peppers open-side up on a baking sheet. These are your mouse bodies. Place one strand of cooked spaghetti in each pepper half. Leave about 4 inches of the strand hanging out of the pepper, to look like a tail.

6. Add a few spoonfuls of the cheese filling to each pepper. Set two pretzels on top of each pepper half to look like legs. Add one more spoonful of filling to cover the pretzels' centers.

Crispy Mice continued next page

6

TIP

Serve your mice with a side of ranch dressing or hot sauce for some extra flavor.

Crispy Mice, continued

7 Put 1 cup of flour in a small bowl. Whisk the eggs and milk together in a separate bowl. In a third bowl, stir together the breadcrumbs, 1 cup flour, ½ teaspoon salt, and ½ teaspoon ground pepper.

8 Coat a clean baking sheet in cooking spray. Then coat one pepper mouse in cooking spray. Carefully dip the mouse in the flour bowl, and use clean hands to coat it with flour. Next dip the mouse in the egg and milk mixture. Finally coat the mouse in the breading mixture, and set it feet-side down on a baking sheet. Repeat with the remaining mice, and refrigerate for 1 hour.

9 Preheat the oven to 375°F. Coat the grill rack with cooking spray, and place the rack in the baking pan.

10 Arrange the mice feet-side down on the grill rack. Bake for 30 to 45 minutes.

11 Remove the pan from the oven, and let it cool for 10 minutes.

12 Arrange the mice on a serving plate, and tell guests to gobble them up before they scurry away!

WRAPPING UP

Cleaning Up

Once you are done cooking, it is time to clean up! Make sure to wipe up spills, wash dishes, and clear the table. Wash and put away any props you used that don't belong in the kitchen. Make sure any leftovers are properly packaged and refrigerated.

Keep Cooking!

Let the foul party foods you made inspire you! Think of ways to put new, terrifying twists on the recipes you tried. Or dream up new ideas for gag-worthy party dishes. Think gross, and keep on cooking!

GLOSSARY

batter: a thin mixture containing flour, eggs, oil, or other ingredients that is used to make baked goods

boil: to heat a liquid until it gives off steam and bubbles

broil: to cook by exposing a food directly to a heat source

capers: pickled flower buds often used in cooking

dash: a very small amount

edible: safe to eat

flush: even or level with something

garnish: to decorate food before serving it

jicama: a starchy root vegetable native to Mexico that can be eaten cooked or raw

knead: to work, press, and fold dough with one's hands until it is smooth

latex: a substance used to make some rubber products

lukewarm: a little bit warm

marinade: a sauce in which food is soaked to make it more flavorful

minced: chopped or cut into very small pieces

pimientos: sweet peppers that are often chopped into small pieces and stuffed into olives

preheat: to heat an oven to the required temperature before putting in the food

Glossary continued on next page

reinforce: to strengthen something by adding more material

sanitize: to clean something so it is free of germs

sauté: to fry in a bit of butter or oil

savory: smelling and tasting good

simmer: to cook something in water that is not quite boiling and has very small bubbles

steamer: a container in which food is cooked using steam

template: a shape that can be used as a guide to making the same shape

tentacle: a long, flexible limb on some animals, such as jellyfish, octopuses, or squid

translucent: almost clear

whisk: to stir very quickly using a fork or a tool made of curved wire

vegetarian: without meat

PHOTO ACKNOWLEDGMENTS

Recipe photographs are by Mighty Media, Inc. Additional photographs are used with permission of: © Pressmaster/Shutterstock Images, p. 4; © Elena Elisseeva/Shutterstock Images, p. 6; © darkscott/iStockphoto, p. 7; © Pressmaster/Shutterstock Images, p. 8; © Tomwang112/iStockphoto, p. 30; © Axel Alvarez/Shutterstock Images, p. 52; © Yuri_Arcurs/iStockphoto, p. 74; © Aldo Murillo/iStockphoto, p. 96; © Jason Lugo/iStockphoto, p. 118; © Fertnig/iStockphoto, p. 140.

Lerner Publications Company
A division of Lerner Publishing Group, Inc.
241 First Avenue North
Minneapolis, MN 55401 USA

For reading levels and more information, look up this title at www.lernerbooks.com.

Main body text set in Tw Cen MT Std.
Typeface provided by Monotype.

Library of Congress Cataloging-in-Publication Data

Names: Vega, Ali, author.
Title: Hideously delicious recipes that disgust and delight / by Ali Vega.
Description: Minneapolis : Lerner Publications, [2019] | Series: Little kitchen of horrors | Audience:
Age: 7–11. | Audience: Grades 4 to 6.
Identifiers: LCCN 2018002499 (print) | LCCN 2018007257 (ebook) | ISBN 9781541529120 (eb pdf) |
ISBN 9781512449907 (lb : alk. paper) | ISBN 9781512448948 (pb : alk. paper)
Subjects: LCSH: Desserts—Juvenile literature. | Cooking—Juvenile literature. | Food craft—
Juvenile literature. | LCGFT: Cookbooks.
Classification: LCC TX733 (ebook) | LCC TX733 .V46 2019 (print) | DDC 641.86—dc23

LC record available at https://lccn.loc.gov/2018002499

Manufactured in the United States of America
1-42821-26497-2/8/2018